150 best
desserts
in a jar

150 best
desserts
in a jar

Andrea Jourdan

Robert
ROSE

For complete cataloguing information, see page 214.

Disclaimer
The recipes in this book have been carefully tested by our kitchen and our tasters. To the best of our knowledge, they are safe and nutritious for ordinary use and users. For those people with food or other allergies, or who have special food requirements or health issues, please read the suggested contents of each recipe carefully and determine whether or not they may create a problem for you. All recipes are used at the risk of the consumer.

We cannot be responsible for any hazards, loss or damage that may occur as a result of any recipe use.

For those with special needs, allergies, requirements or health problems, in the event of any doubt, please contact your medical adviser prior to the use of any recipe.

Design and Production: Kevin Cockburn/PageWave Graphics Inc.
Editor: Judith Finlayson
Copyeditor: Gillian Watts
Proofreader: Gillian Watts
Indexer: Gillian Watts
Photography: Philip Jourdan
Food Styling: Francesca Jourdan
Prop Styling: AF Gourmet
Prop Credits: AF Gourmet

Cover image: Cantaloupe and Raspberry Splash (page 148)

We acknowledge the financial support of the Government of Canada through the Book Publishing Industry Development Program (BPIDP) for our publishing activities.

Published by Robert Rose Inc.
120 Eglinton Avenue East, Suite 800, Toronto, Ontario, Canada M4P 1E2
Tel: (416) 322-6552 Fax: (416) 322-6936
www.robertrose.ca

Printed and bound in USA.

1 2 3 4 5 6 7 8 9 CKV 21 20 19 18 17 16 15 14 13

Philip, this one is for you
and you know why.

Contents

Acknowledgments

If you ask me what I liked best as a child, it's easy: I loved watching my dad, a pastry chef, turn the magic pink paste from a pastry bag into sugar roses to decorate cakes. He was a champion and a magician. First he mixed the sugar and color, then he piped out little flowers that looked like full blooms on the table. When I think about that, I realize that my father gave me much more than the techniques and discipline needed for pastry making. He also passed on his sheer love for detail and his appreciation of taste. He used to say that confections must be delicious because taste memory lasts longer than visual memory — for which, fortunately, we have cameras. There are no sugar roses in this book, but I hope you will find a bit of my dad's legacy.

When my publishers asked me to write a book on desserts in jars, I accepted on the spot. It has indeed been a great pleasure. I hope that everyone who uses this book will not only try the recipes themselves but pass them on to others.

That is what cookbooks are for — sharing the joys of the table.

I have to thank my publishers, Erwan Leseul and Bob Dees, for giving me this amazing opportunity and for allowing me such scope for creativity. Words of appreciation go to my editors, Emilie Mongrain, who patiently held my hand and kept me on schedule and to Judith Finlayson for her role in the English-language edition of this book. To friends, family and kitchen assistants who helped to test the recipes, I am enormously grateful. It has been a fantastic journey.

As usual, a thank-you to my daughter, Francesca, for assisting me in managing my ever-growing stack of recipes in so many different languages (and, of course, for her assistance with tasting). I also thank my husband, Philip, for keeping me on my toes and for being so patient. Also, thanks to everyone who passed on recipes to me over the years so I could transform them into lots and lots of delicious desserts in jars. Sharing is what it's all about — and jars do that best.

Introduction

I have always loved jars. There are so many different sizes and shapes and they sparkle so beautifully when freshly washed. Keeping jars used to be part of our tradition. They often found a second life as containers for buttons or nails or were saved to fill with homemade jams or pickles. Today we can't make preserves in recycled jars because safety concerns demand proper jars that protect against breakage and contamination. But we can save pretty and unusual jars, substituting them for more conventional dishes in which to serve a wide variety of delicious desserts. And though I've developed virtually all of the recipes in this book with readily available Mason-type jars in mind, when I make my own desserts, I love to serve them in some of the old jars I have saved for many years.

Nowadays, using recycled jars — or those intended for home preserving — as serving vessels has become something of a trend. It is routinely done in restaurants all over the world to make a statement. Jars have become part of restaurants' "table staging." It is their variation of the staging process people now use when selling their homes, wherein professional decorators advise them on using plates, platters and glassware to establish the appropriate ambiance for their target audience.

Not only are tasting menus built around small portions that lend themselves to being served in elegant little jars, clear glass jars are perfect vessels for showing off trendy "deconstructed" recipes — for instance, a barley soup in three parts: broth in one jar, cooked barley in another, and a mixture of prepared herbs on a porcelain spoon. It is up to you, the diner, to reconstruct the dish in the process of enjoying it.

I see chefs all over the world buying into this frenzy. In Chicago, Chef Martial Noguier of Bistronomic serves some of his James Beard Award–nominated dishes in small jars, and GT Fish & Oyster presents its celebrated chowders in jars. I currently live in Montreal, where the renowned pastry chef Patrice Demers has been serving his justifiably famous chocolate, caramel and Maldon salt *pot de crème* in a Mason jar for years. The list goes on and on. Today, even New York's illustrious Eleven Madison Park serves dishes in Mason jars from time to time. There is no telling where this trend will stop. The French pastry genius Pierre Hermé has gone even further, by serving desserts in used sardine tins! Creativity has no limits.

When you serve dessert in a jar, the enthusiastic response is amazing. Everyone wants to try your creation. Serving jars are a great way to put a different spin on a familiar recipe or to present something new and unusual. In addition to recycled jars and traditional preserving jars, you can now buy elegant European-designed jars and even drinking jars, which are ideal for serving fluid desserts such as sweet soups.

So start saving jars that you find particularly pretty and watch for unusual jars when you visit kitchen stores. Jars should not be hidden away in the cupboard. They should be filled with delicious desserts waiting to be presented in style at your table.

— *Andrea Jourdan*

Ten Key Points for Making Desserts in a Jar

1. The jar sizes indicated in the recipes are only a suggestion: you can use larger or smaller jars or even recycled jam or condiment jars in some recipes. Just be sure to divide the contents equally among the jars. Also, if your dessert is being baked, pay attention to the cooking time. It will vary depending upon the volume of the content and how it is distributed within the jar. The thickness of the glass will also have an impact on cooking time.

2. Never use jars that are cracked or chipped. Not only are they unsightly, they may not be safe. Be very cautious when using recycled jars in general. Do not use them for baking or freezing, as they are susceptible to breaking at high or low temperatures.

3. Always use jars that are practical to fill and to eat from. Remember that a layered dessert will require a taller jar than a creamy flan.

4. Think creatively and serve a recipe in a variety of jars. I sometimes serve the same dessert to each guest in a different jar.

5. Use a funnel, ice-cream scoop or pastry bag to help you fill the jars neatly.

6. In the oven, always place a baking sheet under the jars. When cooking in a bain-marie (a baking pan filled with water), separate the jars well so they do not come in contact with each other and are surrounded by water.

7. If you have a convection function on your oven, turn it off. If it can't be turned off, reduce the baking temperature by 25°F (14°C). Always bake in the center of a preheated oven, unless otherwise instructed.

8. When removing jars from the oven, always leave them on the baking sheet until they have cooled, unless otherwise specified.

9. If you are freezing your dessert in a jar, be sure to leave extra space at the top — food expands when frozen. If using lids, cover the jar with plastic wrap before placing the lid on the jar.

10. If you are giving a dessert in a jar as a gift, always label it with the date to make sure it is used within the appropriate time frame.

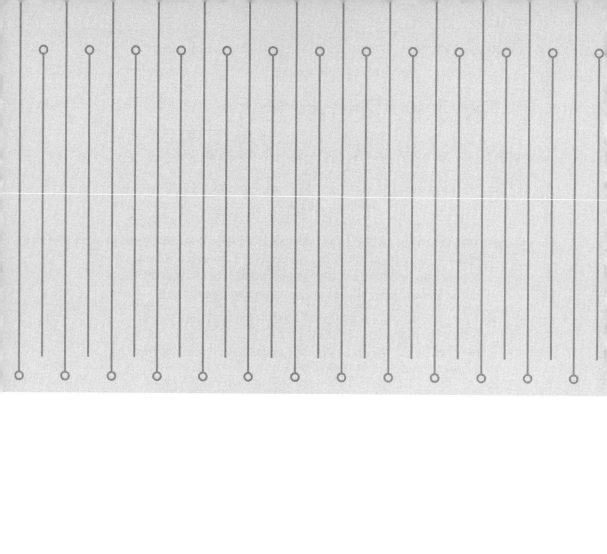
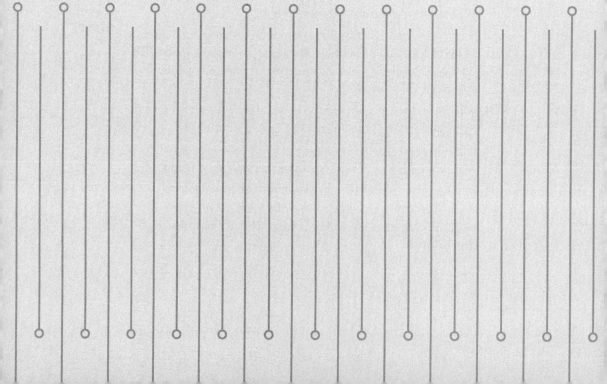

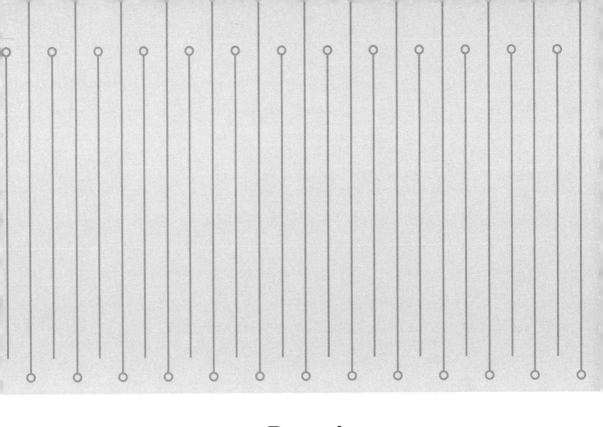

Part 1

Warm and Comforting

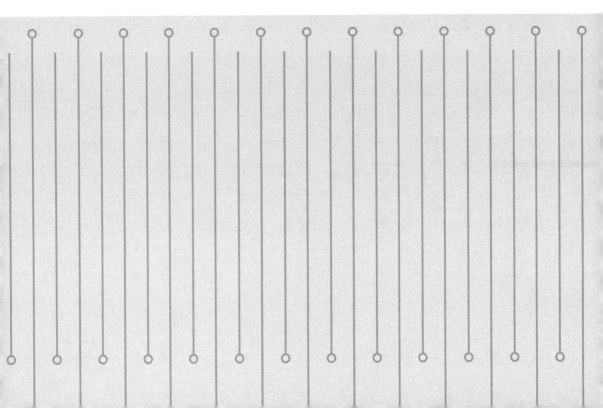

Crumbles, Cobblers and Other Fruit Desserts

Apple and Green Peppercorn Crumble

Don't you just love the fresh, piquant flavor of green peppercorns! Have you ever had them paired with apples? The combination is simply superb. And since apple crumble seems to be the most enjoyed fall dessert (at least in our family), it seemed natural to bring them together. Here is a variation of my sister's favorite apple crumble: unusual but delicious.

Tip

Use cooking apples such as Cortland: they do not brown when peeled and retain their shape when cooked.

- Preheat oven to 350°F (180°C)
- Six 8-ounce (250 mL) wide-mouth jars
- Rimmed baking sheet, lined with parchment paper

FRUIT

6	apples, cored and diced	6
3 tbsp	granulated sugar	45 mL
1/4 cup	water	60 mL
1 tbsp	drained green peppercorns in brine, crushed	15 mL

CRUMBLE

1/4 cup	all-purpose flour	60 mL
1/2 cup	packed brown sugar	125 mL
1/2 cup	crushed pretzels	125 mL
1/4 cup	large-flake (old-fashioned) rolled oats	125 mL
1/4 cup	cold unsalted butter, cut into cubes	60 mL

1. *Fruit:* In a saucepan, combine apples, sugar and water. Cook over low heat for 8 minutes, stirring often. Mix in green peppercorns and cook for 3 minutes. Transfer to jars, dividing equally. Place on prepared baking sheet.

2. *Crumble:* In a bowl, combine flour, brown sugar, pretzels and rolled oats. Add butter and mix with fingertips until texture is crumbly.

3. Add crumble mixture to jars, dividing equally. Transfer to preheated oven and bake for 30 minutes or until top is golden brown and filling is bubbly. Remove from oven and serve immediately.

Pear and Almond Crumble

Although they originated in Asia, pears were one of the first fruits to be brought to North America from Europe. They are one of the more aromatic fruits and they create elegant desserts. In this recipe, they pair particularly well with almonds and just a hint of ginger.

Tip

Choose pears that are firm to the touch and very aromatic, with smooth skins. Store unripe pears in a paper bag at room temperature for a few days to ripen. Always peel pears before cooking, as their skin tends to become tough when cooked.

- Preheat oven to 400°F (200°C)
- Four 8-ounce (250 mL) wide-mouth jars, buttered
- 2 rimmed baking sheets, lined with parchment paper
- Electric mixer

FRUIT CUSTARD

2	pears, peeled, cored and cut into quarters	2
6 tbsp	melted butter	90 mL
4	large eggs	4
¾ cup	heavy or whipping (35%) cream	175 mL
⅓ cup	granulated sugar	75 mL
1½ tbsp	all-purpose flour	22 mL
1 tbsp	brandy	15 mL
¼ tsp	almond extract	1 mL

CRUMBLE

10	gingersnap cookies, crushed	10
¼ cup	packed brown sugar	60 mL
¼ cup	sliced almonds	60 mL
¼ cup	melted butter	60 mL

1. *Fruit Custard:* Place pears on a prepared baking sheet. Using a pastry brush, brush with melted butter. Transfer to preheated oven and bake for 15 minutes or until fork-tender. Remove from oven and set aside until cool enough to handle. Reduce oven heat to 300°F (150°C).

2. Meanwhile, in a large bowl, using mixer at medium speed, beat eggs, cream, sugar, flour, brandy and almond extract until smooth, about 6 minutes. Set aside.

3. *Crumble:* In another bowl, combine gingersnaps, brown sugar, almonds and melted butter. Using your fingers or a pastry blender, combine until moist clumps form.

4. *Assembly:* Place 2 pieces of pear in each jar. Pour egg mixture overtop, dividing equally. Place jars on baking sheet, spacing apart, and bake in preheated oven for 15 minutes. Remove from oven and top each jar with crumble mixture, dividing equally. Return to oven and bake for 20 minutes, until custard sets and top is golden. Remove from oven and set aside to cool for 10 minutes before serving.

Nutmeg-Spiked Peach and Blueberry Cobbler

When I was a little girl and still my grandma's princess, we went together to gather tiny blueberries in her extended backyard (30 acres of woods behind her garden, where we often saw rabbits, deer and bears). I didn't pick a lot because they stained my fingers, but I remember carrying the baskets, enjoying the perfume of the fruit on hot days and eating a lot of blueberries, which my grandmother made into marvelous cobblers. Late-summer favorites, blueberries and peaches remain delicious partners, especially when cooked under a rich, tasty blanket. Here's a tribute to my grandma's delightful garden.

Tips

This makes 10 servings because, in my opinion, cobblers should always be prepared for a crowd.

Blueberries are best at the end of summer, when the tiny, succulent wild ones are available.

- Preheat oven to 375°F (190°C) and place racks in upper third
- Ten 8-ounce (250 mL) wide-mouth jars
- Rimmed baking sheet, lined with parchment paper

FRUIT

¾ cup	granulated sugar	175 mL
3 tbsp	cornstarch	45 mL
6	peaches, pitted and sliced	6
2 lbs	blueberries	1 kg
2 tsp	vanilla extract	10 mL
2 tbsp	freshly squeezed lemon juice	30 mL

TOPPING

1½ cups	all-purpose flour	375 mL
4 tbsp	packed brown sugar, divided	60 mL
½ cup	large-flake (old-fashioned) rolled oats	125 mL
½ tsp	baking powder	2 mL
2 tsp	ground nutmeg	10 mL
Pinch	salt	Pinch
3 tbsp	cold unsalted butter, cut into cubes	45 mL
⅔ cup	buttermilk	150 mL

1. *Fruit:* In a large bowl, whisk together sugar and cornstarch. Add peaches, blueberries, vanilla extract and lemon juice; toss to combine. Divide filling evenly among jars (fill to three-quarters to leave room for the topping).

2. *Topping:* In a large bowl, mix flour, 3 tbsp (45 mL) brown sugar, rolled oats, baking powder, nutmeg and salt. Using your fingers, rub in butter until mixture resembles coarse meal. Add buttermilk and stir just until a dough forms. Drop dough onto fruit, dividing equally. Sprinkle with remaining brown sugar, dividing equally.

Tips

You can leave the peel on the peaches, as it is more rustic and helps to keep the peach flesh from becoming too mushy.

Use jars that are larger or smaller than those called for, to suit what you have available. Just be sure to leave room for the topping and divide both components equally among the jars. Adjust the baking time accordingly.

Make Ahead

These cobblers can be made 2 days ahead, covered with aluminum foil and refrigerated. Reheat for 10 minutes in a 300°F (150°C) oven.

The cobblers can also be frozen uncooked and cooked later. Allow the frozen cobbler to stand at room temperature for 30 minutes. Cook at 325°F (160°C) for about 35 minutes.

3. Transfer jars to prepared baking sheet. Bake in preheated oven for 35 minutes or until fruit is bubbling and topping is golden brown. Remove from oven and cool for 15 minutes before serving.

Variations

Peach and Raspberry Nutmeg Cobbler: Substitute an equal quantity of raspberries for the blueberries.

Double Blueberry Nutmeg Cobbler: Skip the peaches and double the quantity of blueberries.

Double Peach Nutmeg Cobbler: Skip the blueberries and double the peaches — but that would be an insult to my grandma!

Apricots and Peaches under a Blanket

This is a very quick way to make a pie in summer when peaches and apricots arrive at the market. Although apricots might look like little peaches, they taste quite different. This recipe offers a combination of slightly tart apricots and the sweetness of fragrant peaches. This is sure to be a winning summer treat.

Tips

Use a round cookie cutter that is wider than the opening of your jars, or the rim of a glass or an appropriately sized glass lid.

If you can't find peach syrup, use an equal quantity of peach nectar and add 1½ tsp (7 mL) granulated sugar.

Choose peaches that are a little soft and without bruises.

Apricots should have a deep orange color and be a little soft. Like peaches, they should have a fresh aroma.

- Preheat oven to 375°F (190°C)
- Four 8-ounce (250 mL) wide-mouth jars
- Rimmed baking sheet, lined with parchment

BLANKET

8 oz	puff pastry, thawed	250 g

FRUIT

2 tsp	unsalted butter	10 mL
1 tbsp	packed brown sugar	15 mL
4	apricots, halved and pitted	4
2	peaches, halved and pitted	2
1 tsp	ground cardamom	5 mL
¼ cup	peach syrup (see Tips, left, and on page 96)	60 mL
1	egg yolk, beaten with 1 tbsp (15 mL) water	1
2 tsp	granulated sugar	10 mL

1. *Blanket:* On a lightly floured surface, roll puff pastry into a 10-inch (25 cm) square about ⅛ inch (3 mm) thick. Using a cookie cutter, cut out circles just a little larger than the openings of the jars. Place circles flat on a plate with plastic wrap in between and refrigerate.

2. *Fruit:* In a skillet, melt butter. Add brown sugar and stir over low heat until melted. Add apricots and peaches. Sprinkle with cardamom and cover. Cook for 2 minutes. Remove from heat. With a spoon, roll fruit in the caramel in the pan. Transfer 2 pieces of apricot and 1 piece of peach to each jar. Pour 1 tbsp (15 mL) peach syrup into each jar.

3. *Assembly:* Place 1 circle of dough on each jar. Using your fingertips, pinch dough all around and tuck inside jar. With a small knife, make a cross in the top of the dough. Brush with egg wash and sprinkle with sugar.

4. Place jars on prepared baking sheet, spacing apart, and bake in preheated oven for 20 to 25 minutes or until top is golden and puffed up. Remove from oven and serve immediately.

Apple and Orange Cobbler

A basket of sun-kissed apples, a cool breeze and falling leaves mean it's time for apple cobbler. The cobbler is a truly North American dessert dating back at least to the 18th century. It is the homiest of desserts, but although it looks humble, its flavors can be quite sophisticated. Here is my quick version. Served in a jar, this is so cute!

Tips

Use homemade or store-bought pie dough, thawed if frozen. A refrigerated 9-inch (23 cm) pre-rolled pie crust works just fine.

To make orange segments, use a sharp knife to remove the peel and white pith. Holding the fruit over a bowl to catch the juices, cut along either side of the white membranes to remove the segments.

Use apples suited for baking, such as Golden Delicious, Cortland or Royal Gala.

The baking time will reflect the variety of apples used. Some take a bit longer than others.

- Preheat oven to 350°F (180°C)
- Four 8-ounce (250 mL) wide-mouth jars, buttered

FRUIT

2	oranges	2
3	apples, peeled, quartered and cut into thick slices	3
½ cup	granulated sugar	125 mL
½ tsp	ground cinnamon	2 mL
1 tbsp	freshly squeezed orange juice	15 mL
1 tsp	cornstarch	5 mL
¼ cup	sweetened condensed milk	60 mL

TOPPING

8 oz	pie dough (see Tips, left)	250 g
1	large egg yolk, beaten with 1 tbsp (15 mL) whipping (35%) cream	1

1. *Fruit:* Using a rasp grater, zest the oranges. Peel, then cut into segments (see Tips, left).

2. In a bowl, combine orange zest and segments and apples. Add sugar, cinnamon, orange juice and cornstarch. Mix gently.

3. Pour 1 tbsp (15 mL) condensed milk into each jar. Transfer fruit mixture to prepared jars.

4. *Topping:* On a lightly floured surface, roll out dough to approximately ¼ inch (0.5 cm) thick. Cut out 8 square pieces (approximately 2 inches/10 cm each), smaller than the mouths of the jars. Place 2 pieces of dough in each jar, overlapping but leaving the edges open so the filling can bubble around the topping. Brush dough with egg wash.

5. Place jars on a baking sheet. Bake in preheated oven for 25 to 35 minutes (see Tips, left) or until topping is golden and mixture is bubbly. Remove from oven and serve immediately.

Poached Apples with Calvados

Some of my happiest culinary memories are from the Normandy region of France, where I spent numerous summers. That's where I first realized the level of dedication that farmers bring to their jobs, and where I learned to use apples in many different recipes. This one was passed on to me by a good friend who makes Livarot, a soft, aromatic cow's-milk cheese, and who never refuses a little glass of Calvados. The sheer essence of life in Normandy is in this recipe.

Tip

Although Camembert is produced in Normandy, it can be replaced by Brie in this recipe. You can make the slices as thick as you like.

• Four 12-ounce (375 mL) wide-mouth jars

4	apples, peeled and cored	4
¼ cup	granulated sugar	60 mL
4 tbsp	salted butter	60 mL
½ tsp	ground cinnamon	2 mL
2 cups	unsweetened apple juice	500 mL
¼ tsp	nutmeg	1 mL
4	slices Camembert cheese (see Tips, left)	4
1 cup	Calvados	250 mL

1. Cut apples into quarters and place in a bowl. Sprinkle with sugar and stir to coat.

2. In a saucepan, melt butter over medium heat. Add apples and cook, stirring often, for 4 minutes. Add cinnamon, apple juice and nutmeg and cook for 5 minutes, shaking the pan often. Remove from heat. Using a slotted spoon, transfer fruit to jars, dividing equally. Set syrup aside.

3. Place a slice of Camembert in each jar to cover the apples.

4. Return saucepan to stovetop and bring apple syrup to a boil; boil for 2 minutes. Add Calvados, stir well and remove from heat.

5. Pour syrup over apples and cheese and serve immediately.

Moroccan-Style Date and Apricot Couscous

Makes 8 servings

I adore couscous served any way, but these light and tender grains lend themselves very well to dessert. This recipe is based on a traditional way to serve sweet couscous, with dried fruits and spices. The scented grains will make you feel as if you are in a tent in the desert. Enjoying food from exotic places is an incredibly efficient way to travel the world.

Tips

A traditional element of Middle Eastern cooking, orange blossom water (or orange flower water) is a natural extract made from bitter oranges (such as Seville) in a process of steam distillation. It can be found in specialty food stores, Middle Eastern food shops and some supermarkets.

Substitute an equal quantity of vanilla-flavored or plain yogurt for the crème fraîche.

- Eight 8-ounce (250 mL) jars

2 cups	instant couscous	500 mL
2 tbsp	unsalted butter, cubed	30 mL
2 cups	boiling orange juice	500 mL
2 tbsp	granulated sugar	30 mL
1 tbsp	ground cinnamon	15 mL
2 tsp	ground cardamom	10 mL
1 cup	chopped pitted dates	250 mL
1 cup	chopped dried apricots	250 mL
	Small fresh mint leaves	
2 tbsp	orange blossom water (see Tips, left)	30 mL
4 tbsp	crème fraîche (see Tips, left)	60 mL

1. Place couscous in a bowl and add butter cubes, arranging evenly overtop. Add boiling orange juice and mix quickly. Cover and set aside for 5 minutes.

2. In a small bowl, mix sugar, cinnamon and cardamom. Add to couscous, stirring with a fork to break up any clumps and to fluff. When mixture is at room temperature, add dates and apricots and mix well.

3. Transfer to jars, dividing equally. Garnish each jar with a few mint leaves and drizzle with orange blossom water, dividing equally. Top each jar with a dollop of crème fraîche and serve immediately.

Steamed Puddings and Bread Puddings

Spiced Pumpkin Flash

The spiced-up pumpkin purée makes a perfect dessert, and not only for Thanksgiving. It offers a comforting flavor all year long, especially during the cold winter months.

Tips

To make pumpkin purée from scratch, cut a ripe pie pumpkin in half and scoop out the seeds and stringy fibers. Lay the pumpkin halves face down on a baking sheet lined with parchment paper. Bake at 350°F (180°F) until soft, about 1½ hours. Cool, scoop out the flesh and purée in a food processor with 3 tbsp (45 mL) granulated sugar. Pumpkin purée can be frozen. Thaw before using.

Making your own purée produces the best results, but in a pinch you can use canned pumpkin purée. Just make sure it is not pumpkin pie filling, which has added ingredients.

- Preheat oven to 350°F (180°C)
- Six 8-ounce (250 mL) wide-mouth jars
- Baking pan large enough to accommodate the jars

4	small raisin or cinnamon buns	4
2 tbsp	cornstarch	30 mL
1 cup	heavy or whipping (35%) cream	250 mL
3	egg yolks	3
½ cup	granulated sugar	125 mL
2 cups	pumpkin purée (see Tips, left)	500 mL
⅛ tsp	crushed red pepper flakes	0.5 mL
⅛ tsp	ground cinnamon	0.5 mL
¼ tsp	ground ginger	1 mL
⅛ tsp	ground nutmeg	0.5 mL
⅛ tsp	ground allspice	0.5 mL
⅛ tsp	ground cloves	0.5 mL

TOPPING

1 cup	sour cream	250 mL
2 tbsp	packed brown sugar	30 mL
⅛ tsp	crushed red pepper flakes	0.5 mL

1. Cut buns horizontally into ½-inch (1 cm) slices. Using a cookie cutter or the top of a glass, cut pieces of buns to the size of the jar openings.

2. In a bowl, combine cornstarch and cream. In a large bowl, whisk egg yolks and sugar until pale. Whisk in pumpkin purée, red pepper flakes, cinnamon, ginger, nutmeg, allspice and cloves. Add cornstarch mixture and whisk until well combined.

3. Place 1 slice of raisin bun on the bottom of each jar. Cover with half the pumpkin mixture, dividing equally. Place another slice of bun in each jar and top with remaining pumpkin mixture, dividing equally. Cover with foil. Place jars in baking pan, spaced evenly apart and not touching the sides of the pan, and add enough water to come halfway up the sides of the jars.

4. Transfer to preheated oven and bake for 30 to 40 minutes.

5. *Topping:* In a bowl, whisk together sour cream, brown sugar and red pepper flakes.

6. Remove jars from oven and transfer to a wire rack to cool for 5 minutes. Spoon topping over the top and serve immediately.

Apricot and Chocolate Chip Pudding

This is a good recipe for introducing your children to the joy of baking. With little supervision they can help you prepare this quick and colorful pudding. It is also a great way to add fruit to their diet.

Tips

Choose the ripest apricots. They should have a deep orange color and a strong, fresh scent. Once harvested, apricots do not continue to mature; they simply go bad slowly.

To avoid splashing boiling water, place the pan filled with jars on the oven rack, then add the water. Slide rack into oven.

- Preheat oven to 350°F (180°C)
- Six 8-ounce (250 mL) wide-mouth jars, buttered
- Electric mixer
- Baking pan large enough to accommodate the jars

1 cup	granulated sugar	250 mL
6	ripe fresh apricots, halved and pitted	6
3	large eggs	3
1 tbsp	packed brown sugar	15 mL
½ cup	sweetened almond milk	125 mL
½ cup	ground almonds	125 mL
½ cup	cake flour	125 mL
½ tsp	baking powder	2 mL
½ cup	chocolate chips	125 mL

1. Place sugar in a saucepan. Add apricots and toss to coat. Cook over low heat, without stirring, for 3 minutes. Remove from heat. Transfer to prepared jars, dividing equally.

2. In a bowl, using electric mixer at medium speed, beat eggs and brown sugar until frothy. At low speed, beat in almond milk. Fold in ground almonds, flour and baking powder. Fold in chocolate chips. Spoon over apricots, dividing equally. Cover tops with aluminum foil.

3. Place jars in baking pan spaced evenly apart and not touching the sides of the pan, and add enough water to come halfway up the sides of the jars. Bake in preheated oven for 1 hour. Be sure to check the water level frequently and, if necessary, add more water so the pan never becomes dry.

4. Remove from oven and let cool in pan for 5 minutes before serving.

Christmas Pudding

**Makes
10 servings**

I am a big fan of preparing food gifts for the holidays, and this is one of the best gifts I have ever made. This pudding is dark, sticky and dense — certainly not light! — and everyone appreciates the time and effort it takes. Double the recipe and tie a beautiful red ribbon around the jars. 'Tis the season to be generous!

Tips

Do not be put off by the list of ingredients — it is easy to make this pudding! Suet might be the only ingredient that is difficult to find; try going to your local butcher and he may give it to you for free. Do not get bird-grade suet! Vegetarian suet is made from palm oil and either rice or wheat flour; it is available in specialty stores.

- Preheat oven to 325°F (160°C)
- Ten 4-ounce (125 mL) jars, buttered
- Parchment paper
- Kitchen twine
- Baking pan large enough to accommodate the jars

2 cups	mixed dried fruit (golden raisins, raisins, currants)	500 mL
1 cup	fresh breadcrumbs	250 mL
1/2 cup	shredded suet, beef or vegetarian (see Tips, left)	125 mL
1/2 cup	dark brown sugar	125 mL
1/4 cup	chopped almonds	60 mL
2 tbsp	chopped candied lemon peel	60 mL
1	apple, peeled, cored and finely chopped	1
2 tbsp	finely grated orange zest	30 mL
1/4 cup	freshly squeezed lemon juice	60 mL
1 cup	brandy, divided	250 mL
1/2 cup	milk	125 mL
1/2 cup	self-rising flour, sifted (see Tips, page 29)	125 mL
1 tsp	ground allspice	5 mL
1 tsp	ground cinnamon	5 mL
2	large eggs	2
2 tbsp	shredded dried coconut	30 mL
6 tbsp	heavy or whipping (35%) cream	90 mL

1. In a large bowl, combine dried fruit, breadcrumbs, suet, brown sugar, almonds, candied peel, apple, orange zest and lemon juice. Add half the brandy and stir well. Pour in milk. Cover with plastic and refrigerate overnight.

2. Sift flour, allspice and cinnamon into another large bowl. Add fruit mixture and mix well.

3. In a small bowl, beat eggs lightly. Add to fruit mixture, beating rapidly (it should have a fairly soft consistency). Fold in coconut.

4. Spoon into prepared jars, pressing down gently with the back of a spoon. Cover with a double layer of parchment paper placed directly on the surface. Cover top of each jar with aluminum foil and tie securely with kitchen twine.

Tips

If you don't have self-rising flour, substitute ½ cup (125 mL) all-purpose flour, ¾ tsp (3 mL) baking powder and ¼ tsp (1 mL) salt.

Use jars that are smaller or larger, to suit your needs. The important thing is to leave a little space at the top so the pudding can expand a bit when it cooks.

5. Place jars in baking pan, spaced evenly apart and not touching the sides of the pan, and add enough boiling water to come halfway up the sides of the jars. Cover pan with a large piece of aluminum foil, creating a steamer. Transfer to preheated oven and bake for 3 hours, until puddings are a deep shade of brown. Be sure to check the water level frequently and, if necessary, add more water so the pan never becomes dry.

6. Remove from oven. Transfer jars to wire racks and set aside to cool for 1 hour. Remove covers, including parchment, prick the puddings with a skewer and add remaining brandy, dividing equally. Wipe rims clean. Place fresh parchment over the jars and retie with clean twine. Refrigerate for at least 2 days or up to 10 days.

7. To serve, reheat pudding by placing jars in a vegetable steamer for 20 to 25 minutes. Remove covers. Top with a little whipping cream and serve immediately.

Orange Pudding with Vanilla Meringue

This is a very impressive dessert. It takes a bit of work but it's worth it. The delicious steamed pudding and the fresh vanilla-scented meringue make a memorable end to a special meal.

Tips

If you don't have self-rising flour, substitute 1 cup (250 mL) all-purpose flour, 1½ tsp (7 mL) baking powder and ½ tsp (2 mL) salt.

You will have a lot of extra vanilla meringue. Turn it into cookies. Place in a pastry bag, pipe onto a cookie sheet and bake at 175°F (80°C) for about 2 hours. Store cookies, loosely covered with parchment paper, in a dry place (do not refrigerate). Use them to make sandwich cookies, serve with ice cream or fruit salad, or break them in small pieces and bake into brownie dough.

- Six 8-ounce (250 mL) jars, buttered
- Electric mixer
- Parchment squares cut to fit over tops of jars
- Steamer (see Tips, page 31)

PUDDING

6 tbsp	orange marmalade, divided	90 mL
½ cup	butter, softened	125 mL
½ cup	granulated sugar	125 mL
2 tsp	finely grated orange zest	10 mL
½ tsp	ground ginger	2 mL
2	eggs	2
1 cup	self-rising flour (see Tips, left)	250 mL
¼ cup	orange juice	60 mL
¼ cup	buttermilk	60 mL
¼ cup	diced dried apricots	60 mL
	Boiling water	

SYRUP

½ cup	orange juice	125 mL
¼ cup	orange liqueur	60 mL
½ cup	granulated sugar	125 mL
2	small oranges, peeled and segmented (see Tips, page 21)	2

VANILLA MERINGUE

2	large egg whites	2
1 cup	granulated sugar	250 mL
¼ cup	water	60 mL
1 tsp	vanilla extract	5 mL

1. *Pudding:* Place 1 tbsp (15 mL) orange marmalade in bottom of each prepared jar.

2. In a large bowl, using electric mixer at medium speed, beat butter, sugar, orange zest and ginger until light and fluffy. Add eggs one at a time, beating after each addition until incorporated. Sift flour over mixture and beat at low speed until blended. Add orange juice and buttermilk and beat at low speed until blended. Fold in apricots.

Tip

If you do not have a large steamer, place jars in a large, deep baking pan, lined with a tea towel folded in half (so you have 2 layers). Pour boiling water halfway up the jars and cover with a double sheet of foil. Place on stovetop over low heat and cook for 50 minutes. Check often to make sure water level is always halfway up the jars, and add hot water as needed.

3. Spoon mixture into prepared jars, filling halfway. Cover each jar with a piece of parchment paper and secure with elastic bands or kitchen twine. Pierce a small hole in each cover.

4. Set jars on a steamer placed in a large saucepan (see Tip, left). Carefully pour boiling water into saucepan to halfway up the sides of the jars. Cover pan tightly. Place over medium heat and bring to a boil. Reduce heat to very low and simmer for 50 minutes. Check often to make sure water level is always halfway up the jars, and add hot water as needed.

5. *Syrup:* Meanwhile, in a saucepan, combine orange juice, orange liqueur and sugar. Cook over medium heat, stirring, for 3 minutes or until sugar dissolves. Reduce heat to low. Simmer for 5 minutes or until thick and syrupy. Remove from heat. Add orange segments and roll them around in syrup. Set aside.

6. *Vanilla Meringue:* In a large, heatproof bowl placed over a pot of simmering water, combine egg whites, sugar, water and vanilla. Using electric mixer with clean beaters, beat at low speed until mixture is warm and sugar has dissolved. Beat at high speed for about 10 minutes, until thick and fluffy. Remove from heat and continue beating meringue for 8 minutes.

7. Remove steamer from heat. Carefully lift insert from water. Remove jars and place on a wire rack; cool for 5 minutes. Carefully wipe jars and remove paper covers. Spoon syrup over puddings, dividing equally. Top each with a spoonful of vanilla meringue and serve immediately.

Steamed Strawberry Pudding with Strawberry Sauce

This recipe, an elegant temptation, is inspired by Judith Finlayson's recipe in *175 Essential Slow Cooker Classics*. It makes a relatively low-calorie dessert that still tastes very rich. All her recipes give us a new, fantastic vision of how to use our slow cookers better. She convinced me to get my slow cooker out of the cupboard . . . and it's never going back in.

Tip

Be certain to follow the instructions when a recipe calls for adding eggs one at a time and mixing well after each addition. If you add the eggs all at once, the mixture might separate.

- Six 8-ounce (250 mL) tall jars, buttered
- Electric mixer
- Large (minimum 6 quart) oval slow cooker

PUDDING

1/3 cup	unsalted butter, softened	75 mL
1/4 cup	granulated sugar	60 mL
4	large eggs, separated	4
3/4 cup	all-purpose flour	175 mL
2 cups	sliced hulled fresh strawberries	500 mL

SAUCE

1/4 cup	granulated sugar	60 mL
1/4 cup	water	60 mL
2 cups	sliced hulled strawberries	500 mL
1 tbsp	balsamic vinegar	15 mL

1. *Pudding:* In a bowl, using electric mixer at medium speed, whisk butter and sugar until light and fluffy. Mix in egg yolks one at a time, beating until each is incorporated. Gradually add flour, beating until well incorporated. Fold in strawberries.

2. In another bowl, using electric mixer at high speed, beat egg whites until stiff peaks form. Gently fold into batter. Pour into prepared jars. Cover each jar with a piece of parchment paper and a sheet of aluminum foil and secure with kitchen twine or an elastic band.

3. Place jars in slow cooker. Add enough boiling water to come 1 inch (2.5 cm) up the sides of the jars. Cover and cook on High for about 1 1/2 hours, until a toothpick inserted in middle of cake comes out clean. Remove from stoneware and transfer to a wire rack.

This is a great recipe to make when strawberries are in season, plentiful and inexpensive.

4. *Sauce:* In a saucepan, combine sugar and water. Bring to a boil for 1 minute. Add strawberries and bring to a boil. Cook for several minutes, until strawberries start to lose their juices. Remove from heat and mix in balsamic vinegar. Serve strawberry pudding warm, with warm sauce on the side.

Variations

The strawberries can be replaced by an equal quantity of raspberries or blueberries, fresh or frozen.

If using blueberries, replace the balsamic vinegar in the sauce with 1 tbsp (15 mL) freshly squeezed lemon juice.

Banana Pudding with Salted Caramel Sauce

This is a dreamlike dessert to end any dinner beautifully.

Tips

If you don't have self-rising cake flour, substitute 1¾ cups (425 mL) sifted all-purpose flour, ⅓ cup (75 mL) cornstarch, 1 tbsp (15 mL) baking powder and 1 tsp (5 mL) salt. Sift the combined ingredients twice before using.

Be certain to follow the instructions when a recipe calls for adding eggs one at a time and mixing well after each addition. If you add the eggs all at once, the mixture might separate.

- Preheat oven to 350°F (180°C)
- Eight 8-ounce (250 mL) wide-mouth jars, buttered
- Baking pan large enough to accommodate the jars
- Blender
- Electric mixer

PUDDING

2 cups	self-rising flour (see Tips, left)	500 mL
½ tsp	baking powder	2 mL
1 cup	unsalted butter, divided	250 mL
3	ripe bananas, mashed	3
½ tsp	ground aniseed	2 mL
1 tsp	baking soda	5 mL
1 cup	packed light brown sugar	250 mL
2	large eggs	2
1 tsp	vanilla extract	5 mL
3 tbsp	dried cranberries	45 mL

SALTED CARAMEL SAUCE

2 cups	packed dark brown sugar	500 mL
½ cup	salted butter	125 mL
½ cup	rum	125 mL
¼ cup	corn syrup	60 mL
½ tsp	ground nutmeg	2 mL
2 cups	heavy or whipping (35%) cream	500 mL
1 tsp	vanilla extract	5 mL
⅛ tsp	fine sea salt	0.5 mL

1. *Pudding:* In a bowl, combine flour and baking powder. Set aside.

2. In a small skillet, melt 1 tbsp (15 mL) butter. Add bananas and aniseed. Cook over medium heat, stirring, for 2 minutes. Transfer to blender. Add baking soda and blend for 30 seconds. Set aside to cool.

3. In a bowl, using electric mixer at medium speed, beat remaining butter and brown sugar until pale and fluffy. Add eggs one at a time, beating after each addition until incorporated. Add reserved banana and flour mixtures and vanilla. Beat until smooth. Fold in cranberries. Spoon mixture into prepared jars, dividing equally. Cover loosely with aluminum foil and poke a few holes in the foil.

Tips

Use bananas that are ripe but still a bit firm.

If you don't have aniseed, substitute $\frac{1}{4}$ tsp (1 mL) ground fennel seeds. This will give the pudding a different taste, but nonetheless an interesting one.

4. Place jars in baking pan, spaced evenly apart and not touching the sides of the pan, and add enough water to come halfway up the sides of the jars. Bake in preheated oven for 25 to 30 minutes or until a toothpick inserted in the center comes out clean. Remove from oven and transfer jars to a wire rack to cool slightly.

5. *Salted Caramel Sauce:* Meanwhile, in a saucepan, combine brown sugar, butter, rum, corn syrup and nutmeg. Bring to a boil over low heat, stirring until sugar has dissolved. Whisk in cream, vanilla and salt. Simmer over low heat for 10 minutes or until sauce is sticky and thick. Serve pudding warm, topped with warm sauce.

Chocolate and Hazelnut Pudding

My friend Roberto loves hazelnuts. My friend Roberto also loves chocolate. I love steamed puddings. It is only natural, when we get together, that I prepare this little treat. It's so delicious.

Tips

For best results, use very good quality chocolate and fresh hazelnuts.

If your jars don't have lids, use pieces of aluminum foil, bringing the foil 1 inch (2.5 cm) down the sides of each jar. Tie securely with kitchen twine.

When steaming on the stovetop, it's always a good idea to line the bottom of the pan with a folded towel, which helps to insulate the jars from the heat of the stove and prevent them from bouncing around.

- Eight 8-ounce (250 mL) wide-mouth jars, with lids (see Tips, left)
- Electric mixer
- Roasting pan large enough to accommodate the jars, preferably with lid

PUDDING

1 cup	packed brown sugar	250 mL
1/3 cup	butter, softened	75 mL
2	eggs	2
2/3 cup	chopped dark (70%) chocolate, melted	150 mL
1 tbsp	cold coffee	15 mL
1 tsp	finely grated orange zest	5 mL
1 1/2 cups	ground hazelnuts, divided	375 mL
1 cup	all-purpose flour	250 mL
1/3 cup	unsweetened cocoa powder	75 mL
3/4 cup	milk, divided	175 mL

SAUCE

1/3 cup	granulated sugar	75 mL
1/3 cup	water	75 mL
1/2 cup	chopped bittersweet chocolate	125 mL
1 cup	chopped hazelnuts	250 mL

1. *Pudding:* In a large bowl, using electric mixer at medium speed, beat sugar and butter until fluffy. Add eggs one at a time, beating after each addition until incorporated. Add melted chocolate, coffee and orange zest; beat for 1 minute.

2. In another bowl, combine hazelnuts, flour and cocoa. Using a spatula, fold into butter mixture in two batches, alternating with milk.

3. Pour batter into jars and smooth out tops. Place circles of parchment directly on batter surface. Place lids on jars and secure loosely.

Make Ahead

Complete Step 4. Remove jars from steamer, cool completely, wrap tightly in plastic and refrigerate for up to 1 week. To reheat in microwave, remove plastic and metal lids or aluminum foil covers, and the parchment covering the puddings. Working in two batches, cover puddings with a large microwave-safe bowl. Reheat on High until hot, 3 to 5 minutes, depending on the power of your microwave. Cool for 5 minutes before serving.

4. Place jars on a rack in roasting pan, spaced evenly apart and not touching the sides of the pan, and add enough hot water to come halfway up sides of jars. Cover pan with aluminum foil and, if possible, a lid (otherwise use a second sheet of aluminum foil). Place on stovetop and steam for 1 hour over medium heat or until edges of puddings pull away from sides of jars. Check the level of water often, adding hot water as necessary to maintain level.

5. *Sauce:* Meanwhile, in a saucepan, combine sugar and water. Bring to a boil over medium heat. Stir in chocolate and boil over high heat for 2 minutes. Remove from heat. Pour half the sauce into a pitcher and fold in hazelnuts. Set remainder aside.

6. Remove jars from steamer and transfer to a wire rack. Set aside until cool enough to handle. Remove lids and parchment from jars. Brush puddings with reserved plain chocolate sauce. Serve puddings warm, with chocolate-hazelnut sauce on the side.

Lemon Pudding with Raspberry Sauce

Some recipes are worth keeping and passing on to family and friends. This recipe crossed the ocean and arrived one day in my kitchen. Make it yours, transform it by adding your favorite berries, and then pass it on to someone else who will appreciate it.

Tips

Use jars that are larger or smaller than those called for, to suit what you have available. Just be sure to divide the batter equally and allow plenty of room for expansion when it cooks. Also pay attention to the cooking time, which may need to be adjusted.

These pudding cakes can be refrigerated for up to 2 days. Complete Steps 1 through 4 and cover. Allow to sit at room temperature for 30 minutes before serving with hot raspberry sauce.

- Preheat oven to 300°F (150°C)
- Six 8-ounce (250 mL) jars, buttered
- Electric mixer
- Baking pan large enough to accommodate the jars

3	large eggs, separated	3
2 tbsp	unsalted butter, softened	30 mL
1 cup	granulated sugar	250 mL
3 tbsp	all-purpose flour	45 mL
3 tbsp	finely grated lemon zest	45 mL
Pinch	salt	Pinch
½ cup	freshly squeezed lemon juice	125 mL
½ cup	whole milk, at room temperature	125 mL
SAUCE		
1 lb	fresh raspberries	500 g
2 tbsp	light corn syrup	30 mL

1. In a large bowl, using electric mixer at medium speed, beat egg whites until they form soft peaks. Set aside.

2. In another bowl, using electric mixer at medium speed, beat butter and sugar until fluffy, about 3 minutes. Reduce speed and add egg yolks one at a time, mixing after each addition until completely incorporated. Add flour, lemon zest and salt and beat at low speed until combined. Add lemon juice and milk and beat until incorporated. Using a rubber spatula, fold in beaten egg whites.

3. Pour batter into prepared jars, dividing equally and filling halfway. Place jars in baking pan, spaced evenly apart and not touching the sides of the pan, and add enough boiling water to come halfway up the sides of the jars.

4. Transfer to preheated oven and bake for 30 minutes. Remove from oven and transfer jars to a wire rack to cool. When jars are cool enough to handle, using an apple corer or a small round cookie cutter, cut out and remove the center of each cake.

5. *Sauce:* In a saucepan, combine raspberries and corn syrup. Cook over medium heat, stirring constantly, for 7 minutes. Remove from heat. Pour over pudding and serve immediately.

Blackberry Bread Pudding

Makes 6 servings

Bread pudding is a truly luscious dessert with limitless possibilities. In this version, sinfully delicious fresh blackberries enhance the pleasure. Brace yourself — this dessert is just too good.

Tips

Thick-sliced white bread or challah can replace the raisin bread in this recipe, but they will not give the same scrumptious taste.

Frozen blackberries can replace the fresh ones.

This is a generous serving of pudding, but not as ample as it might seem, because the bread soaks up the liquid and expands when cooked. However, by all means use 8- or 10-ounce (250 or 300 mL) jars if you prefer. Just make sure they have a wide opening, and divide the preparation equally among them. Also pay attention to the cooking time, which may need to be adjusted accordingly.

- Preheat oven to 350°F (180°C)
- Six 12-ounce (375 mL) jars, buttered (see Tips, left)
- Rimmed baking sheet, lined with parchment
- Electric mixer
- Baking pan large enough to accommodate the jars

1	large (16 oz/500 g) loaf raisin bread, crusts removed and cut into 1-inch (2.5 cm) cubes	1
4	large eggs	4
1 cup	granulated sugar	250 mL
2 cups	heavy or whipping (35%) cream	500 mL
2 cups	table (18%) cream	500 mL
1 tsp	vanilla extract	5 mL
Pinch	salt	Pinch
2 cups	fresh blackberries, divided	500 mL
6 tbsp	crème fraîche	90 mL

1. Place bread cubes on prepared baking sheet and bake in preheated oven for 10 minutes or until light golden. Remove from oven and set aside to cool.

2. In a large bowl, using electric mixer at high speed, whisk eggs, sugar, heavy and table creams, vanilla and salt. Add bread cubes and toss gently. Cover with a clean tea towel and set aside to soak for 30 minutes.

3. Pour half the bread mixture into prepared jars, dividing equally. Cover with half of the blackberries, dividing equally. Repeat.

4. Place jars in baking pan, spaced evenly apart and not touching the sides of the pan, and add enough hot water to come halfway up the sides of the jars. Bake in preheated oven for 25 to 35 minutes or until puddings are set and golden on top. Remove jars from pan and transfer to a wire rack to cool slightly. Top each jar with a dollop of crème fraîche and serve immediately.

Apple, Apricot and Vanilla Bread Pudding

Once in the hills of northern Italy, in the Trentino region, I came upon a strange and delightful restaurant. The floors of this exquisite establishment had been painted with poems about wine and food. I had never walked on words before, and it was a fascinating experience. The chef was one of those rare people who have a magic touch with desserts. When I tasted his bread pudding, I did not have enough words to express my joy. Since then we have been exchanging recipes — as in times long past, when people wrote letters to maintain long-distance friendships. Here is one of those simple recipes. Enjoy!

Tip

Always use soft fresh vanilla beans. The dried ones are old and difficult to cut open. Used vanilla pods can be rinsed, dried and placed in a large bowl of granulated sugar. Cover and store and you will always have vanilla sugar on hand.

- Eight 8-ounce (250 mL) jars, buttered and sprinkled with sugar
- Electric mixer
- Baking pan large enough to accommodate the jars

1¼ cups	granulated sugar	300 mL
1	vanilla bean, split lengthwise and scraped, pod and seeds set aside (see Tip, left)	1
6	large eggs	6
1 cup	heavy or whipping (35%) cream	250 mL
1 cup	milk	250 mL
¼ tsp	kosher or coarse sea salt	1 mL
½ tsp	vanilla extract	2 mL
3 cups	crustless white bread cubes (½ inch/1 cm)	750 mL
5	baking apples, peeled and shredded	5
8 tbsp	apricot preserves	120 mL

1. In a bowl, mix sugar with reserved vanilla seeds. Place 1 tsp (5 mL) of this vanilla sugar in bottom of each jar.

2. In a bowl, using electric mixer at medium speed, beat eggs and remaining vanilla sugar until fluffy. Slowly add cream, milk, salt and vanilla extract, beating at low speed. Fold in bread cubes and apples. Cover bowl with a clean tea towel and set aside for 15 minutes to soak.

3. Preheat oven to 350°F (180°C). Transfer apple mixture to prepared jars, filling halfway. Drop 1 tbsp (15 mL) apricot preserve into center of each jar.

4. Place jars in baking pan, spaced evenly apart and not touching the sides of the pan, and add enough hot water to come halfway up the sides of the jars. Bake in preheated oven for 25 to 35 minutes or until puddings are set and tops are golden. Remove from oven and serve immediately.

Old-Fashioned Bread Pudding with Crunchy Pecans

As long as we have bread, we will have dessert. I remember coming home from school in a snowstorm and being surprised by the incredible aroma of bread pudding. That made it worthwhile to go to school. My sister and I took off our boots and coats in frenzy to get to the kitchen as fast as we could. No need for words — nothing says "welcome home" better than a warm pudding.

Tip

Store pecans in the refrigerator for up to 6 months.

- Preheat oven to 350°F (180°C)
- Four 12-ounce (375 mL) wide-mouth jars, buttered
- Rimmed baking sheet, lined with parchment paper

2 cups	milk	500 mL
3	eggs, beaten	3
1/3 cup	granulated sugar	75 mL
1/2 tsp	salt	2 mL
1/2 tsp	vanilla extract	2 mL
1/2 cup	packed dark brown sugar	125 mL
1/2 cup	chopped pecans	125 mL
1 tsp	cinnamon	5 mL
1/2 tsp	nutmeg	2 mL
4	thick slices white bread, crusts removed, broken into small pieces	4

1. In a saucepan over low heat, heat milk until hot but not boiling.

2. In a bowl, whisk eggs, sugar and salt. Gradually whisk half the hot milk into the egg mixture. Add remaining milk and vanilla extract, whisking constantly.

3. In a small bowl, combine brown sugar, pecans, cinnamon and nutmeg.

4. Place bread pieces in buttered jars, dividing equally. Add half the pecan mixture, dividing equally. Top with egg mixture. Cover with remaining pecan mixture. Place jars on baking sheet, spacing apart.

5. Bake in preheated oven for 35 minutes or until a toothpick inserted near the center comes out almost clean. Remove from oven and serve immediately.

Brown Sugar Bread Pudding

Makes 6 servings

In my childhood we always had bread pudding for dessert at Aunt Louise's house. The silky bread, the subtle hints of vanilla and cinnamon, the sexy touch of whisky in the sauce, the gooey maple syrup — they all sang the harmony of simple pleasures. A plus was Aunt Louise's secret ingredient: pure love. Here is my version of her masterpiece.

Tips

If you have leftover brioche, use it to replace the bread. It's even better.

Bread pudding is best served warm, but it can be kept refrigerated, tightly covered, for up to 2 days (if you can resist).

Leftover sauce can be kept refrigerated for up to 1 week. Serve it with ice cream, pancakes or waffles.

- Preheat oven to 325°F (160°C)
- Six 8-ounce (250 mL) jars, buttered
- Electric mixer
- Baking pan large enough to accommodate the jars

PUDDING

2 cups	half-and-half (10%) cream	500 mL
1/4 cup	unsalted butter	60 mL
1 1/4 cups	packed dark brown sugar	300 mL
4	eggs	4
1 tsp	cinnamon	5 mL
1 tsp	vanilla extract	5 mL
2 cups	cubed (1/2 inch/1 cm) baguette	500 mL

SAUCE

3 tbsp	salted butter	45 mL
1/2 cup	maple syrup	125 mL
1/2 cup	confectioner's (icing) sugar	125 mL
1/4 cup	whisky	60 mL
1/2 cup	heavy or whipping (35%) cream	125 mL

1. *Pudding:* In a saucepan over medium heat, heat cream for 4 minutes. Add butter, stirring until melted. Set aside.

2. In a large bowl, using electric mixer at medium speed, beat brown sugar, eggs, cinnamon and vanilla for 2 minutes. Reduce speed to low and mix in reserved cream mixture.

3. Place bread cubes in prepared jars, dividing equally. Pour batter overtop, filling jars to two-thirds. Place jars in baking pan, spaced evenly apart and not touching the sides of the pan, and add enough hot water to come halfway up the sides of the jars. Bake in preheated oven for 35 minutes or until pudding is set.

Tip

To avoid splashing boiling water, place the pan filled with jars on the oven rack, then fill with the water. Slide rack into oven.

4. *Sauce:* While puddings are baking, melt butter in a saucepan. Remove from heat. Add maple syrup, confectioner's sugar and whisky, stirring until incorporated. Add cream and whisk until smooth.

5. Turn off oven. Remove jars from oven and pan. Add sauce, dividing equally. Return jars to oven, placing directly on rack and leaving the door open. Let stand for 15 minutes in oven before serving. Serve warm.

Cranberry Red Currant Crumb Pudding

Makes 6 servings

This is a great recipe from Judith Finlayson's book *175 Essential Slow Cooker Classics*. As with all her recipes in this must-have book, it is easy to prepare and brings out the natural flavors of good home cooking. This one might quickly become one of your family's favorites.

Tip

Never throw out leftover bread. It can be used to prepare delicious desserts.

- Large (minimum 6 quarts) oval slow cooker
- Six 8-ounce (250 mL) tall jars, buttered

2 cups	whole milk	500 mL
¾ cup	granulated sugar	175 mL
2 tbsp	unsalted butter	30 mL
2 cups	fresh breadcrumbs	500 mL
3	large eggs	3
1 tsp	vanilla extract	5 mL
¼ tsp	salt	1 mL
¼ cup	dried cranberries	60 mL
3 tbsp	red currant jelly, stirred until smooth	45 mL

1. In a saucepan over medium heat, combine milk, sugar and butter. Bring to a boil, whisking until butter has melted. Remove from heat and mix in breadcrumbs.

2. In a bowl, whisk eggs, vanilla and salt. Fold in cranberries and ¼ cup (60 mL) of the breadcrumb mixture. Add remaining breadcrumb mixture and mix well.

3. Divide red currant jelly equally among prepared jars. Add batter, dividing equally. Cover each jar with a piece of parchment and a piece of aluminum foil. Secure with kitchen twine or an elastic band. Place jars in slow cooker and pour in enough boiling water to come 1 inch (2.5 cm) up the sides of the jars. Cover and cook on High for 1 hour or until a toothpick inserted in the middle of cakes comes out clean. Remove from slow cooker and allow to cool for at least 15 minutes or cool completely before serving.

Queen of Puddings

This is a regal traditional treat. It comes from times gone by, when every bit of bread had to be used, so the crumbs were saved to be soaked in milk for making desserts. If you were lucky enough to have jam to put in your pudding, I guess the result was fit to be called a Queen.

Tip

Let the egg whites come to room temperature before beating, to ensure maximum volume in your meringue.

- Preheat oven to 350°F (180°C)
- Six 8-ounce (250 mL) jars, buttered
- Electric mixer
- Rimmed baking sheet, lined with parchment paper

6 tbsp	raspberry jam	90 mL
1 cup	half-and-half (10%) cream	250 mL
1 cup	heavy or whipping (35%) cream	250 mL
1½ tsp	vanilla extract	7 mL
5	large egg yolks	5
1¼ cups	granulated sugar, divided	300 mL
1 cup	fresh breadcrumbs	250 mL
3 tbsp	finely grated lemon zest	45 mL
5	egg whites	5
1 tbsp	confectioner's (icing) sugar	15 mL

1. Place 1 tbsp (15 mL) raspberry jam in bottom of each jar. Set aside.

2. In a saucepan over low heat, combine half-and-half, heavy cream and vanilla. Bring to a gentle boil. Remove from heat.

3. In a large bowl, using electric mixer at medium speed, whisk egg yolks and ¾ cup (175 mL) sugar until pale and thick. Whisking constantly, slowly add warm cream mixture. Fold in breadcrumbs and lemon zest. Pour into jars, dividing equally, and place on baking sheet, spacing apart.

4. Bake in preheated oven for 20 to 25 minutes or until pudding has risen and is almost set but still slightly wobbly. Remove from oven and transfer jars, on baking sheet, to a wire rack. Set aside to cool.

5. Increase oven temperature to 400°F (200°C).

6. In a large, clean bowl, using electric mixer with clean beaters at high speed, beat egg whites to soft peaks. Beat in remaining granulated sugar 1 tbsp (15 mL) at a time, beating to stiff peaks. Add a thick layer of the mixture to each jar. Sprinkle tops with confectioner's sugar. Return jars to hot oven and bake for 7 minutes or until meringue is crisp and lightly browned. Remove from oven and serve immediately.

Creamy Custards, Flans and Creams

Kiwi and Strawberry Flan

I refer to this dessert
as my jar of vitamins.
Kiwis are known for
providing abundant
potassium and vitamins
C, E and A. Don't tell
the kids — let them
think this dessert is
just, well, delightful.

Tip

For a different effect,
use yellow kiwis and
add 1 tsp (5 mL)
additional sugar when
whisking the eggs.

- Preheat oven to 350°F (180°C)
- Four 8-ounce (250 mL) jars, buttered
- Baking pan large enough to accommodate the jars

4	kiwifruit, peeled (see Tips, left)	4
¼ cup	unbleached all-purpose flour	60 mL
¼ cup	cornstarch	60 mL
Pinch	salt	Pinch
3	eggs	3
½ cup	granulated sugar	125 mL
¾ cup	sour cream	175 mL
3 tbsp	strawberry jam	45 mL
½ tsp	vanilla extract	2 mL

1. Cut each kiwi into thin slices and place in the bottom of each jar.

2. In a bowl, combine flour, cornstarch and salt.

3. In a large bowl, whisk eggs and sugar until foamy. Gradually whisk in flour mixture. Mix in sour cream, jam and vanilla. Pour over kiwis, dividing equally.

4. Place jars in baking pan, spaced evenly apart and not touching the sides of the pan, and add enough hot water to come halfway up the sides of the jars. Bake in preheated oven for 30 minutes or until flan is no longer wobbly. Remove from oven. Transfer to a wire rack and cool for 5 minutes before serving.

Warm Orange-Spiked Cranberry Custard

Close your eyes and imagine tart cranberries floating in a pool of sweet, soft, silky custard that fills your mouth with warm pleasure. Now wake up, hurry to the kitchen and prepare this recipe!

Tip

Most commercially produced dried cranberries contain added sugar. If using organic unsweetened cranberries, add 1 tbsp (15 mL) sugar to the recipe.

- Preheat oven to 350°F (180°C)
- Six 8-ounce (250 mL) jars, buttered
- Electric mixer
- Baking pan large enough to accommodate the jars

3	large egg yolks	3
½ cup	granulated sugar	125 mL
2 tbsp	all-purpose flour	30 mL
1 cup	heavy or whipping (35%) cream	250 mL
¼ cup	cranberry juice	60 mL
3 tbsp	finely grated orange zest	45 mL
3	large egg whites	3
Pinch	salt	Pinch
½ cup	dried cranberries (see Tip, left)	125 mL
1 tbsp	confectioner's (icing) sugar	15 mL

1. In a large bowl, using electric mixer at medium speed, whisk egg yolks and sugar until light and fluffy. Add flour and beat until incorporated. Gradually beat in cream, cranberry juice and orange zest.

2. In another bowl, using electric mixer with clean beaters at high speed, beat egg whites and salt until soft peaks form. Using a whisk, fold into flour mixture (the batter will be very liquid). Fold in cranberries. Pour into prepared jars, dividing equally.

3. Place jars in baking pan, spaced evenly apart and not touching the sides of the pan, and add enough hot water to come halfway up the sides of the jars. Bake in preheated oven for 20 minutes or until custard is lightly browned and center is still wobbly.

4. Remove from oven and sprinkle with confectioner's sugar. Serve immediately.

Puffed Rice and Marshmallow Cream

This is a recipe for the traveler in you. It uses Indian spices to create a marshmallow cream unlike anything your guests have tasted before.

Tips

Garam masala is an Indian mixture of spices. It is readily available in specialty stores.

Marshmallow cream, or fluff, is an American invention from the early 19th century; it contains corn syrup, sugar syrup, dried egg whites and vanilla flavoring. You can make fluff from scratch by mixing, at high speed for 7 minutes, 3 large egg whites, 2 cups (500 mL) corn syrup and a pinch of salt. Add 2¼ cups (550 mL) sifted confectioner's sugar and 2 tsp (10 mL) vanilla extract and mix at low speed until blended. Cover and refrigerate for up to 2 days.

- Six 8-ounce (250 mL) jars, buttered
- Electric mixer

3 cups	puffed rice cereal	750 mL
¼ cup	raisins	60 mL
¼ cup	granulated sugar	60 mL
1 tsp	garam masala (see Tips, left)	5 mL
¼ tsp	ground turmeric	1 mL
½ cup	creamy peanut butter	125 mL
2 tbsp	unsalted butter	30 mL
1 cup	marshmallow cream (see Tips, left)	250 mL
2 tbsp	confectioner's (icing) sugar	30 mL
¼ cup	whole milk	60 mL

1. In a bowl, combine puffed rice, raisins, sugar, garam masala and turmeric. Set aside.

2. In another bowl, using electric mixer at low speed, beat peanut butter and butter for 2 minutes. Beat in marshmallow cream and confectioner's sugar. Gradually add milk and beat for 2 minutes. Pour over puffed rice mixture and stir gently to combine. Transfer to jars, dividing equally.

3. Place jars in microwave oven, spacing evenly apart, and microwave on High for 2 minutes, until warm. Serve immediately.

Plum Clafouti

When summer arrives, I start anticipating the arrival of plums in the markets. Yellow or purple, tiny or large, I love them all. But my favorites are the little green Reine Claude and the long purple Quetsche varieties, which are easier to find. A clafouti is traditionally prepared with cherries. However, it can be prepared with all kinds of fresh fruit. This light cake never ceases to amaze my friends, who always love a country-style treat. Serving clafoutis in jars gives the dessert a little *je ne sais quoi* that makes it a bit more elegant.

Tip

I never refrigerate clafouti. In my opinion, it is best eaten hot out of the oven or at most within 3 hours.

Make Ahead

The plums can be prepared 2 days ahead and kept refrigerated. Complete Step 1 and bring plums to room temperature before adding to the recipe.

- Preheat oven to 325°F (160°C)
- Six 12-ounce (375 mL) wide-mouth jars, buttered and sprinkled with sugar
- Baking pan large enough to accommodate the jars
- Rimmed baking sheet

1 cup	prune liqueur or sweet white wine	250 mL
½ cup	water	125 mL
1¼ cups	granulated sugar, divided	300 mL
1	vanilla bean, cut lengthwise, seeds scraped out, pod and seeds reserved	1
2 lbs	firm, ripe purple plums, halved and pitted (about 20)	1 kg
4	large eggs	4
¼ tsp	salt	1 mL
6 tbsp	all-purpose flour	90 mL
1 cup	whole milk	250 mL
1 tbsp	melted unsalted butter	15 mL
2 tsp	finely grated orange zest	10 mL
1 tbsp	confectioner's (icing) sugar	15 mL

1. In a large saucepan, combine prune liqueur, water, ¾ cup (175 mL) sugar and vanilla pod and seeds. Bring to a boil over high heat, stirring, until sugar dissolves. Boil for 3 minutes. Remove from heat and discard vanilla pod. Add plums. Cover, return to element, reduce heat to low and simmer for 8 minutes. Remove from heat. Using a slotted spoon, transfer plums to prepared jars, dividing equally. Set poaching liquid aside. Set plums aside for 30 minutes.

2. In a bowl, whisk eggs, remaining ½ cup (125 mL) sugar and salt until combined. Gradually whisk in flour. Whisk in milk, butter, orange zest and ¼ cup (60 mL) reserved poaching liquid. Pour over plums, dividing equally. Place jars in baking pan and add enough hot water to come halfway up the sides of the jars.

3. Transfer to preheated oven and bake for 20 minutes. Carefully transfer jars to baking sheet and return to oven. Bake for 15 minutes or until edges are puffed and golden. Remove from oven and let cool on a wire rack for 10 minutes. Sprinkle with confectioner's sugar and serve immediately.

Warm Salted Caramel Pudding

Makes 4 servings

Granulated sugar and salt have extremely contrasting tastes that are quite divine when combined. This is a two-part recipe. The first part is a British-type pudding, almost like a cake; the second is soft and creamy. This is an extremely satisfying dessert indeed.

Tips

If you don't have self-rising flour, substitute $\frac{1}{4}$ cup (60 mL) all-purpose flour, $\frac{1}{2}$ tsp (2 mL) baking powder and $\frac{1}{8}$ tsp (0.5 mL) salt.

Fleur de sel is hand-harvested in Europe on the shores of the Atlantic Ocean. Its taste is more complex and much sweeter than table salt. Fleur de sel is used a lot in desserts and is particularly good when paired with chocolate or caramel. It should be kept in a plastic bag to retain its humidity.

- Preheat oven to 325°F (160°C)
- Four 8-ounce (250 mL) jars, buttered and coated with sugar
- Electric mixer
- Strainer
- Rimmed baking sheet, lined with parchment paper

$\frac{1}{2}$ cup	packed brown sugar	125 mL
$\frac{1}{4}$ cup	self-rising flour (see Tips, left)	60 mL
2	eggs	2
2 tbsp	butter	30 mL
$1\frac{1}{2}$ tsp	vanilla extract, divided	7 mL
2 cups	light (15%) cream, divided	500 mL
1 tbsp	cornstarch	15 mL
Pinch	salt	Pinch
$2\frac{1}{4}$ cups	granulated sugar	550 mL
$\frac{1}{4}$ cup	water	60 mL
1 tsp	fleur de sel or other flaky sea salt such as Maldon (see Tips, left and page 53)	5 mL

1. In a bowl, using electric mixer at low speed, beat brown sugar, flour, eggs, butter, and $\frac{1}{2}$ tsp (2 mL) vanilla until thoroughly blended. Increase speed to medium and beat for 3 minutes or until mixture is pale yellow in color.

2. Spoon mixture into prepared jars, filling to two-thirds full and dividing equally. Place jars on baking sheet, spacing apart, and bake in preheated oven for 20 minutes.

3. Meanwhile, in a small bowl, whisk $\frac{1}{2}$ cup (125 mL) cream with cornstarch, remaining vanilla and salt until smooth. Set aside.

4. In a saucepan, combine sugar and water and bring to a boil over medium heat. Cook, without stirring, for 7 minutes or until it reaches a deep amber color. Remove from heat. Standing well back, very slowly whisk in remaining cream. Return to stovetop and whisk over low heat until caramel has combined with cream.

Tip

If fleur de sel or another flaky sea salt is not available, add $\frac{1}{4}$ tsp (1 mL) table salt in Step 6.

5. Gradually whisk reserved cornstarch mixture into caramel. Cook over medium heat for 6 minutes, stirring, until caramel pudding is very thick. Strain pudding through a fine-mesh strainer set over a large bowl.

6. Remove jars from oven. Sprinkle with fleur de sel. Top with caramel pudding and serve immediately.

Amaretto Sabayon

Sabayon is a light custard that is whipped to create an airy texture. Quick and easy to prepare, it is traditionally made with white wine or Marsala, but this version uses almond-flavored liqueur. During the holidays I like to serve a small sabayon as a "first dessert" and then go on to something more substantial.

Tips

Amaretti are crunchy Italian cookies made of almonds and egg whites. Look for them in specialty food stores.

The sabayon must not get too hot or it will become grainy. That is why the saucepan of boiling water should be removed from the heat as soon as the mixture is placed over it.

If you do not have 6-ounce (175 mL) jars, use 8-ounce (250 mL) jars (which will make 4 servings) or small wineglasses.

- Six 6-ounce (175 mL) jars (see Tips, left)
- Electric mixer

8	egg yolks	8
⅓ cup	granulated sugar	75 mL
¼ tsp	almond extract	1 mL
1¼ cups	almond-flavored liqueur, such as amaretto	300 mL
12	amaretti cookies, crushed (see Tips, left)	12

1. Fill a saucepan halfway with water and bring to a boil over high heat.

2. In a stainless steel bowl, using electric mixer at medium speed, beat egg yolks, sugar and almond extract until pale. Set the bowl over the boiling water. Remove from heat (see Tips, left). Continue beating while slowly adding the liqueur. Beat for 5 minutes or until foamy and light.

3. Place a layer of amaretti cookies in the bottom of each jar, dividing equally. Top with sabayon, dividing equally. Serve immediately.

Variations

Orange Sabayon: Substitute the almond-flavored liqueur with an orange-flavored liqueur such as Cointreau, Triple Sec or Grand Marnier.

This sabayon can also be served as a warm sauce over baked apples or pears.

Kiwi Sabayon with Fruit Salad

Makes 6 servings

Could it be true, as legend has it, that in the 16th century an army of hungry soldiers could commandeer only eggs, sugar and wine from the peasants near Reggio Emilia in Italy? They cooked these ingredients into a warm "soup," and they loved it so much that, after taking the city, they wanted to eat it again. This *zvan bajoun* was their secret weapon; the name was later transformed into *zabaglione*, which in turn became *sabayon* in French. True or not, it is a lovely story.

Tips

Several wines can be used for making sabayon. I like to use Moscato d'Asti, but Marsala is more traditional. Sherry is often used as well, and you can also use ice wine or ice cider.

Kiwi liqueur is produced by combining spirits with natural ingredients such as kiwis and sugar. It is available in well-stocked liquor stores.

- Preheat broiler
- Six 8-ounce (250 mL) jars
- Electric mixer

1 cup	pineapple chunks	250 mL
1 cup	cubed (½ inch/1 cm) mango	250 mL
1 cup	pitted cherries	250 mL
1½ cups	sweet white wine (see Tips, left)	375 mL
8	egg yolks	8
½ cup	granulated sugar	125 mL
¼ tsp	vanilla extract	1 mL
¼ cup	kiwi liqueur (see Tips, left)	60 mL
2	kiwifruit, peeled and diced	2

1. In a bowl, combine pineapple, mango and cherries. Sprinkle with wine and toss well. Cover and set aside at room temperature for 1 hour. Drain, reserving liquid. Transfer fruit to jars, dividing equally. Set liquid aside.

2. Place a large saucepan, half-filled with water, over high heat and bring to boil.

3. In a stainless steel bowl, using electric mixer at medium speed, beat egg yolks, sugar and vanilla until pale and thick. Set bowl over the boiling water and remove from heat (see Tips, page 54). Gradually add reserved soaking liquid, beating constantly. Add kiwi liqueur. Beat at medium speed for 7 minutes or until foamy and light. Fold in kiwis.

4. Pour over fruit in jars. Place jars on a cookie sheet and place under preheated broiler for 2 minutes, until tops are golden. Remove from oven and serve immediately.

Pear and Candied Celery Crème Caramel

Crème caramel is basically vanilla-and-orange-scented custard with a layer of caramel on top. This recipe calls for more egg yolks than whole eggs, giving it the silkiest consistency. Celery is rarely used in a sweet version, but *oh la la*, what a surprise! Its natural sweetness makes it easy to pair with pears. Since both have a delicate flavor, they form a terrific team in your mouth.

Tips

Use pears suitable for cooking, such as Comice, Anjou or Bosc.

If crystals start to form on the sides of the saucepan when you are making the caramel, wipe them down with a brush dipped in cold water.

- Preheat oven to 375°F (190°C)
- Six 8-ounce (250 mL) wide-mouth jars
- Baking dish
- Electric mixer
- Baking pan large enough to accommodate the jars

PEARS AND CELERY

¼ cup	apricot jam	60 mL
½ cup	sweet dessert wine	125 mL
¼ cup	granulated sugar	60 mL
1 tbsp	finely grated lemon zest	15 mL
2	pears, peeled, cored and diced (see Tips, left)	2
4	tender celery ribs, sliced	4

CARAMEL

1 cup	granulated sugar	250 mL
½ cup	water	125 mL

CUSTARD

3 cups	milk	750 mL
1½ tsp	vanilla extract	7 mL
3	eggs	3
4	egg yolks	4
½ cup	granulated sugar	125 mL

1. *Pears and Celery:* In a saucepan, combine apricot jam, wine, sugar and lemon zest. Cook over low heat, stirring, until sugar is dissolved and jam has liquefied. Remove from heat and set aside.

2. Place pears and celery in baking dish. Pour apricot syrup over the top and toss to coat well. Bake in preheated oven for 45 minutes, turning pears and celery twice in their juices. Remove from oven and set aside to cool. Reduce oven heat to 325°F (160°C).

3. *Caramel:* In a heavy saucepan, cook sugar and water, without stirring, until sugar is completely dissolved. When it starts to brown, swirl the saucepan without stirring; this will ensure an even color.

Tips

Cooking custard for too long will result in a tough texture. It is always better to undercook custards a little.

If you have a roasting pan, it will work well as a container for the water bath. To prevent boiling water from splashing when carrying the pan, place pan filled with jars on oven rack before filling. After adding the boiling water, slide rack into oven.

This custard is also good served cold. Let cool for 15 minutes after removing from the oven and refrigerate for at least 2 hours or up to 2 days before serving.

4. When caramel is dark brown, remove from heat and pour into jars, using an oven mitt to hold the jars, dividing equally and swirling to coat evenly. Divide pear mixture evenly among jars. Set aside.

5. *Custard:* In a saucepan over low heat, bring milk and vanilla to a simmer.

6. In a large bowl, using electric mixer at medium speed, beat eggs, egg yolks and sugar until light and foamy. Continue beating while slowly pouring in hot milk mixture. Pour through a fine-mesh sieve into a large measuring cup. Pour into jars, dividing equally (they will be about three-quarters full).

7. Place jars in baking pan, spaced evenly apart and not touching the sides of the pan, and add enough water to come halfway up the sides of the jars. Bake in preheated oven for 45 minutes or until centers are firm but slightly wobbly. Remove from oven. Transfer jars to a wire rack and set aside to cool for 20 minutes.

Almond Milk Pudding

Almond milk has been used as far back as the Middle Ages, appearing in recipes from the 14th century. It can replace regular milk in most recipes. With its velvety texture and delicate crunch, this pudding will not stay on the table for very long.

Tip

Substitute an equal quantity of whole milk for the almond milk and increase the quantity of almond extract to 1 tsp (5 mL).

- Four 8-ounce (250 mL) tall jars
- Electric mixer

1 cup	granulated sugar, divided	250 mL
1 cup	heavy or whipping (35%) cream	250 mL
1 cup	crème fraîche	250 mL
1 cup	plain almond milk (see Tip, left)	250 mL
1/2 tsp	almond extract	2 mL
1/2 tsp	vanilla extract	2 mL
Pinch	salt	Pinch
4	large egg yolks	4
3 tbsp	cornstarch	45 mL
1 cup	sliced almonds	250 mL
1 tbsp	cold unsalted butter, in cubes	15 mL

1. In a saucepan, combine 3/4 cup (175 mL) sugar, cream, crème fraîche, almond milk, almond extract, vanilla and salt. Bring just to a boil over low heat, whisking constantly. Remove from heat and set aside.

2. In a bowl, using electric mixer at medium speed, beat egg yolks and remaining sugar until pale and thick. Beat in cornstarch. Slowly add cream mixture, beating constantly. Return to saucepan over medium heat and cook, stirring constantly with a wooden spoon, for 4 minutes or until thick and glossy. Remove from heat. Add almonds and butter and stir until butter is completely melted.

3. Pour into jars, dividing equally. Serve warm.

Burnt Orange Crème Brûlée

The best crème brûlée I ever tasted was at the now defunct but still memorable Léon de Lyon restaurant in France. I could never reproduce the exact texture and, unfortunately, was never allowed to learn their secret. After years of trying to create the perfect crème brûlée, I finally came up with a recipe that I like enough to share. As for Léon's crème brûlée — well, it might just have been the sweet Muscat wine I drank with it that made it taste so good.

Tip

If you do not have a kitchen torch, preheat broiler. Place jars on baking sheet; sprinkle with a little brown sugar and place under broiler until golden. Remove from oven, sprinkle with remaining brown sugar, top with orange slices and place under broiler for about 2 minutes, until sugar browns to a dark color.

- Preheat oven to 325°F (160°C)
- Four 8-ounce (250 mL) wide-mouth jars, buttered
- Baking pan large enough to accommodate the jars
- Kitchen torch, optional (see Tip, left)

6	large egg yolks	6
½ cup	granulated sugar	125 mL
1½ cups	heavy or whipping (35%) cream	375 mL
⅔ cup	whole milk	150 mL
2 tbsp	finely grated orange zest	30 mL
1 tbsp	orange-flavored liqueur	15 mL
3 tbsp	packed brown sugar, divided	45 mL
1	orange, sliced thinly	1

1. In a bowl, whisk egg yolks and sugar until pale and thick. Set aside.

2. In a saucepan over medium heat, bring cream, milk and orange zest to a simmer. Gradually add to egg yolk mixture, whisking until incorporated. Stir in orange liqueur.

3. Pour custard into prepared jars, dividing equally. Place jars in baking pan, spaced evenly apart and not touching the sides of the pan, and add enough hot water to come halfway up the sides of the jars. Bake in preheated oven for 35 minutes or until center of custards is still wobbly. Remove from oven and transfer jars to a wire rack to cool for 30 minutes. Cover jars with plastic wrap and refrigerate overnight.

4. Place jars on a baking sheet. Sprinkle a little brown sugar over each custard. Using kitchen torch, burn sugar just until it melts. Place orange slices over melted sugar. Sprinkle with remaining brown sugar, dividing equally. Using torch, heat until sugar has caramelized and orange rind is a little burnt. Serve immediately.

Coconut Milk and Curry Crème Brûlée

Is a classic crème brûlée too simple for you? Curry powder, with its warm, spicy aroma, opens up a whole new world of possibilities when used in desserts. Rich and creamy, this exotic dessert is delightfully tempting.

Tips

If you do not have a kitchen torch, the crème brûlée can be placed under the broiler for 2 minutes to caramelize.

To toast the coconut, place unsweetened shredded coconut on a baking sheet and bake in a 350°F (180°C) oven for about 7 minutes, stirring once. Sweetened coconut will toast faster and needs to be checked and stirred more often.

- Preheat oven to 300°F (150°C)
- Six 8-ounce (250 mL) wide-mouth jars
- Electric mixer
- Baking pan large enough to accommodate the jars
- Kitchen torch, optional (see Tips, left)

5	large egg yolks	5
1/2 cup	granulated sugar, divided	125 mL
2 cups	heavy or whipping (35%) cream	500 mL
1 tsp	curry powder	5 mL
1 cup	coconut milk	250 mL
3 tbsp	shredded coconut	45 mL
2 tbsp	packed brown sugar	30 mL
3 tbsp	toasted coconut (see Tips, left)	45 mL

1. In a bowl, using electric mixer at medium speed, beat egg yolks and 1/4 cup (60 mL) granulated sugar until pale and thick.

2. In a saucepan over medium heat, heat cream, curry powder and remaining granulated sugar, stirring, until sugar dissolves and cream just begins to simmer. Add coconut milk and whisk until smooth. Fold in shredded coconut. Whisk into egg mixture. Pour into jars, dividing equally.

3. Place jars in baking pan, spaced evenly apart and not touching the sides of the pan, and add enough water to come halfway up the sides of the jars. Bake in preheated oven for 1 hour or until custards are just set and still a tiny bit wobbly in the center. Remove jars from water and set aside on a wire rack to cool for 1 hour. Refrigerate for at least 3 hours or up to 2 days.

4. Top each custard with 1 tsp (5 mL) brown sugar. Holding a kitchen torch approximately 3 to 4 inches (7.5 to 10 cm) from the surface, caramelize the sugar. Top with toasted coconut, dividing equally, and serve.

Caramel and Cardamom Dip

Caramel has to be my favorite flavor. Good caramel should be thick and have a hint of fresh cream mixed with the bitter taste of darkened sugar.

Tips

This recipe can be varied by using cinnamon or nutmeg instead of cardamom (in the same quantities).

When pouring liquid into caramel, wear oven mitts and a long-sleeved shirt. Caramel is extremely hot and can splatter, especially when you are adding other ingredients.

- Four 8-ounce (250 mL) wide-mouth jars

1 cup	granulated sugar	250 mL
1/4 cup	water	60 mL
1/4 cup	light corn syrup	60 mL
1 cup	heavy or whipping (35%) cream	250 mL
1 cup	sweetened condensed milk	250 mL
5 tbsp	unsalted butter	75 mL
2 tsp	ground cardamom	10 mL
1/2 tsp	fleur de sel	2 mL
8	chocolate wafers	8
8	ladyfingers	8

1. In a saucepan over medium heat, combine sugar, water and corn syrup. Cook, stirring, until sugar dissolves completely. Bring to a boil and cook, without stirring, until mixture is amber, about 5 minutes. Remove from heat. Standing well back, add cream and condensed milk, whisking until incorporated. Return to element and cook, stirring, until bubbly. Remove from heat. Stir in butter, cardamom and fleur de sel.

2. Pour into jars and set aside for 15 minutes to cool. Serve as a dip with chocolate wafers and ladyfingers.

Fudge Cream

I discovered how fantastic and decadent fudge can be in Italy, of all places. In a city in Tuscany there is a great chocolatier named Andrea Slitti, who makes the best spreadable fudge cream in the world (only he does not call it that). To make this extremely rich and sweet concoction as silky as possible, you need to create a good balance among the sugar, butter and milk. When you want to pamper your guests, this is the dessert to have on hand.

Tips

Use your favorite brand of store-bought marshmallow cream. If you prefer to make your own, see Tips, page 50.

Using the best-quality chocolate will make a big difference in the end product.

- Ten 4-ounce (125 mL) jars

1¼ cups	granulated sugar	300 mL
1 cup	prepared marshmallow cream (see Tips, left)	250 mL
2 cups	evaporated milk	500 mL
¼ cup	butter, in pieces	60 mL
	Salt	
7 oz	chopped dark (70%) chocolate	200 g
7 oz	chopped milk chocolate	200 g
3 tbsp	whisky	45 mL
1 tsp	vanilla extract	5 mL
½ cup	chopped walnuts	125 mL
	Wafers or plain cookies	

1. In a large saucepan, combine sugar, marshmallow cream, evaporated milk, butter and salt to taste. Bring to a boil over high heat, stirring constantly. Boil for 3 minutes, until thick and glossy. Remove from heat. Add dark and milk chocolate, stirring until incorporated completely. Stir in whisky and vanilla extract.

2. Pour mixture into jars, dividing equally. Top with chopped walnuts and serve immediately, accompanied by wafers or waffle slices.

Marshmallow Dream

This is one of my family's special treats on Saturday nights. It's a cookie melt that is guaranteed to please everyone with a sweet tooth. Every generation thinks they discovered marshmallows, but this sweet confection was invented by the ancient Egyptians as a medicinal treatment for sore throats.

Tip

I'm not kidding about sore throats. The gelatin binding the sugar in the marshmallow soothes an irritated throat when chewed and swallowed.

- Preheat oven to 300°F (150°C)
- Eight 8-ounce (250 mL) jars, buttered
- Rimmed baking sheet, lined with parchment paper
- Baking pan large enough to accommodate the jars

3 cups	cornflakes	750 mL
¼ cup	milk powder	60 mL
2 tbsp	granulated sugar	30 mL
½ cup	melted butter	125 mL
Pinch	salt	Pinch
8	chocolate chip cookies	8
2 cups	miniature marshmallows	500 mL
½ cup	mini chocolate chips	125 mL
½ cup	dried cranberries	125 mL

1. In a bowl, using your fingers, crush cornflakes. Add milk powder, sugar, butter and salt. Toss to combine. Using your fingers, break up mixture into small clusters. Transfer to prepared baking sheet and bake in preheated oven for 20 minutes. Remove from oven and let cool completely.

2. On a clean work surface, crush cookies with a rolling pin. Transfer to a large bowl. Add cooled cornflake clusters, marshmallows, chocolate chips and cranberries. Toss. Transfer to prepared jars, dividing equally.

3. Place jars in baking pan, spaced evenly apart and not touching the sides of the pan, and add enough hot water to come halfway up the sides of the jars. Bake in preheated oven for 12 minutes or until marshmallows are melted. Remove from oven and serve immediately.

Cakes, Pudding Cakes and Soufflés

Double Chocolate and Chile Pudding Cake

If you have never had chile with chocolate, try it. Mexicans have done it forever. I tasted this concoction in Sicily, where they are also very fond of chile-spiked chocolate. The heat comes only at the end, after the chocolate taste, and it packs a little punch. A splash of heat never hurt anybody — *au contraire!*

Tips

Smoked sweet paprika comes from Spain, where it is called *pimentón*. It is now quite widely available in specialty stores, but if you don't have it, substitute an equal quantity of sweet paprika.

Absolutely do not overbake. This dessert should remain gooey.

- Preheat oven to 350°F (180°C)
- Six 8-ounce (250 mL) wide-mouth jars, buttered
- Baking pan large enough to accommodate the jars

¾ cup	packed brown sugar	175 mL
½ cup	unsweetened cocoa powder	125 mL
1 cup	boiling water	250 mL
¾ cup	all-purpose flour	175 mL
⅓ cup	granulated sugar	75 mL
1 tsp	baking powder	5 mL
½ cup	milk	125 mL
2	eggs, beaten	2
2 tbsp	butter	30 mL
½ tsp	hot pepper flakes	2 mL
1 tsp	vanilla extract	5 mL
½ cup	sour cream	125 mL
1	package (3.9 oz/110 g) instant chocolate pudding mix	1
¾ cup	chocolate chips	175 mL
1	bar (3 oz/100 g) milk chocolate, cut into 6 pieces	1
2 tsp	smoked sweet paprika (see Tips, left)	10 mL

1. In a bowl, whisk brown sugar with cocoa powder. Pour in boiling water and whisk until smooth.

2. In large bowl, whisk together flour, granulated sugar, cocoa mixture and baking powder. Add milk, eggs, butter, chile flakes and vanilla; whisk until well combined.

3. In another bowl, whisk together sour cream and pudding mix. Pour into flour mixture and mix quickly. Fold in chocolate chips.

4. Pour mixture into prepared jars. Place a piece of milk chocolate in the center of each pudding. Place jars in baking pan, spaced apart and not touching the sides of the pan, and add enough hot water to come halfway up the sides of the jars. Bake in preheated oven for 25 to 30 minutes or until cakes are just firm when gently touched but still jiggly in the center. Sprinkle with smoked paprika and serve immediately.

My Grandmother's Blueberry Ginger Cake

I talk a lot about my grandmother's cooking, but she did not actually cook that much. She loved being in her garden, which was full of plants such as rhubarb, raspberries and wild blueberries. Grandma was organized, strict and proud, but she laughed at everything and absolutely loved ginger, so here is a dessert in honor of her memory.

Tips

If you don't have self-rising cake flour, substitute 1¾ cups (425 mL) sifted all-purpose flour, ⅓ cup (75 mL) cornstarch, 1 tbsp (15 mL) baking powder and 1 tsp (5 mL) salt. Sift the combined ingredients twice before using.

To prevent corn syrup or molasses from sticking, first spray the measuring cup with vegetable oil or brush with melted butter.

Crystallized or candied ginger is available at specialty shops and some supermarkets.

- Preheat oven to 325°F (160°C)
- Eight 8-ounce (250 mL) jars, buttered and sprinkled with sugar
- Electric mixer
- Rimmed baking sheet, lined with parchment paper

2¾ cups	fresh blueberries	675 mL
¼ cup	granulated sugar	60 mL
2 cups	self-rising cake flour (see Tips, left)	500 mL
1 tsp	baking soda	5 mL
2 tsp	ground ginger	10 mL
1 tsp	ground cinnamon	5 mL
½ tsp	freshly ground black pepper	2 mL
⅛ tsp	ground cloves	0.5 mL
	Salt	
½ cup	salted butter, at room temperature	125 mL
½ cup	packed light brown sugar	125 mL
2	large eggs	2
½ cup	light corn syrup (see Tips, left)	125 mL
1 cup	milk	250 mL
¼ cup	chopped candied ginger	60 mL
	Vanilla or ginger ice cream, optional	

1. Place jars on a cookie sheet.

2. In a small bowl, combine blueberries and sugar. Transfer to jars, dividing equally.

3. In a bowl, combine flour, baking soda, ginger, cinnamon, pepper, cloves and salt.

4. In another bowl, using electric mixer at medium speed, beat butter and brown sugar until light and fluffy. Beat in eggs one at a time, beating well after each addition. Add corn syrup and beat to combine. At low speed, add flour mixture in two batches, alternating with milk.

5. Pour batter into jars. Divide candied ginger equally among the jars, pushing it slightly into the batter. Place jars on baking sheet, spacing apart.

6. Transfer to preheated oven and bake for about 25 minutes or until a tester inserted in center of cakes comes out clean. Remove from oven and cool on baking sheet for 5 minutes before serving. Serve with a scoop of ice cream, if using.

Chocolate Gingerbread

Chocolate and spices always make a terrific match. Here, this sophisticated combination transforms a childhood favorite into an awesome dessert.

Tips

Don't be intimidated by the long list of ingredients. This is a very easy cake to prepare.

The gingerroot can be replaced by $1\frac{1}{4}$ tsp (6 mL) ground ginger.

To prevent corn syrup or molasses from sticking, first spray the measuring cup with vegetable oil or brush with melted butter.

To avoid splashing boiling water, place the pan filled with jars on the oven rack, then fill with the water. Slide rack into oven.

- Preheat oven to 375°F (190°C)
- Eight 8-ounce (250 mL) wide-mouth jars, buttered
- Electric mixer
- 8 squares parchment, cut to fit tops of jars
- Baking pan with rack, large enough to accommodate the jars

$1\frac{1}{2}$ cups	all-purpose flour	375 mL
3 tbsp	unsweetened cocoa powder	45 mL
$1\frac{1}{4}$ tsp	baking powder	6 mL
$\frac{1}{2}$ tsp	baking soda	2 mL
$\frac{1}{2}$ tsp	salt	2 mL
5 tsp	finely grated peeled gingerroot (see Tips, left)	25 mL
$1\frac{1}{2}$ tsp	ground cinnamon	7 mL
$\frac{1}{4}$ tsp	ground nutmeg	1 mL
$\frac{1}{4}$ tsp	ground cloves	1 mL
$1\frac{1}{2}$ cups	granulated sugar	375 mL
$\frac{1}{4}$ cup	salted butter, at room temperature	60 mL
$1\frac{1}{2}$ tbsp	finely grated orange zest	22 mL
4	large eggs	4
$\frac{1}{2}$ cup	buttermilk	125 mL
$\frac{1}{4}$ cup	molasses	60 mL
$\frac{1}{4}$ cup	dark (64%) chocolate, melted	60 mL
$\frac{1}{4}$ cup	chocolate chips	60 mL
2 tbsp	grated milk chocolate	30 mL

1. In a bowl, combine flour, cocoa, baking powder, baking soda, salt, ginger, cinnamon, nutmeg and cloves.

2. In another bowl, using electric mixer at medium speed, beat sugar, butter and orange zest until pale and fluffy. Add eggs one at a time, beating well after each addition. Beat in buttermilk. Reduce speed to low and add flour mixture in two additions, alternating with molasses. Add melted chocolate and mix well. Fold in chocolate chips.

3. Pour batter into prepared jars. Cover tops with parchment and secure with kitchen twine. Place jars on rack in pan, spacing evenly apart, and add boiling water to come halfway up the sides of the jars. Cover pan tightly with aluminum foil to create a steamer.

4. Lower oven heat to 275°F (140°C). Place pan in oven and steam for $1\frac{1}{2}$ hours or until a tester inserted in center of gingerbread comes out clean. Check often to make sure water level is always halfway up the jars, and add hot water as needed.

5. Remove pan from oven. Transfer jars to a wire rack and set aside to cool for 10 minutes. Remove parchment tops. Sprinkle each jar with a little milk chocolate, dividing equally. Serve warm.

Strawberry Rhubarb Shortcake

This was my real childhood treat! When I had met my dad's expectations at the end of the school year, strawberries would be starting to appear in the market. To celebrate, he would make a giant strawberry shortcake and I could eat all I wanted. Of course it's an old-fashioned, simple dessert but it's also one that everyone in the family enjoyed. And as a bonus, strawberries are loaded with nutrients. Here is Dad's recipe for shortcake, with the addition of rhubarb and served in jars.

Tips

Sifting sugar is something that pastry chefs like to do because it eliminates lumps and aerates the sugar, giving a more uniform texture that benefits certain cakes. You can skip this step if you prefer.

If you prefer, substitute the best sponge cake you can find at the grocery store for the homemade version.

- Preheat oven to 350°F (180°C)
- Six 12-ounce (375 mL) jars (see Tips, page 71)
- 9-inch (23 cm) springform cake pan, lined with buttered and floured parchment paper
- Electric mixer
- Sifter
- Round cookie cutter (see Tips, page 71)

SHORTCAKE

4	large eggs, at room temperature	4
¾ cup	granulated sugar, sifted (see Tips, left)	175 mL
½ tsp	vanilla extract	2 mL
1	vanilla bean, cut lengthwise, seeds scraped out and reserved	1
1 cup	sifted cake flour, divided	250 mL
½ tsp	baking powder	2 mL
Pinch	fine salt	Pinch
⅓ cup	butter, melted	75 mL

STRAWBERRIES AND RHUBARB

½ cup	granulated sugar	125 mL
2 cups	diced rhubarb	500 mL
¼ cup	orange juice	60 mL
1 tbsp	cold water	15 mL
1 tsp	unflavored gelatin	5 mL
1 cup	heavy or whipping (35%) cream	250 mL
¼ cup	confectioner's (icing) sugar	60 mL
½ tsp	vanilla extract	2 mL
3 cups	sliced hulled strawberries (about 1 lb/500 g)	750 mL
6	hulled whole strawberries	6

1. *Shortcake:* In a bowl, using electric mixer at medium speed, beat eggs until foamy. Gradually beat in sugar. Beat until mixture is pale and batter falls in ribbons when beaters are lifted. Fold in vanilla extract and vanilla seeds.

2. Hold sifter (you can use a fine-mesh sieve) over the egg mixture and add half of the already sifted cake flour, half the baking powder and the salt. Sift into egg mixture, then fold in melted butter. Sift and fold in remaining flour and baking powder. Pour batter into prepared pan.

Tips

Use a cookie cutter that is slightly smaller than the interior diameter of the jars.

This recipe can be divided equally into smaller jars or assembled in tall tumblers.

Any leftover rhubarb compote can be used to garnish ice cream, crêpes or waffles or spread on toast.

Make Ahead

The cake can be prepared one day ahead and stored at room temperature, wrapped in plastic.

The rhubarb compote can be prepared up to 3 days ahead. Cover and refrigerate.

3. Lower oven heat to 325°F (160°C). Bake shortcake for 50 minutes or until cake springs back when touched and sides pull away from pan. Remove from oven and let cool in pan for 15 minutes. Remove sides of pan and let cool completely.

4. Using a sharp serrated knife, cut cake in half horizontally. Using cookie cutter (see Tips, left), cut out 12 circles and set aside.

5. *Strawberries and Rhubarb:* In a saucepan, combine sugar, rhubarb and orange juice. Bring to a boil, stirring until sugar has dissolved. Reduce heat and simmer for 20 minutes, stirring often. Remove from heat and set aside to cool for 15 minutes.

6. Pour cold water into a small saucepan. Sprinkle gelatin over the top and set aside for 5 minutes (do not stir). Place saucepan over low heat and stir constantly just until gelatin dissolves. Remove from heat and set aside to cool for 5 minutes.

7. In a large bowl, combine cream, confectioner's sugar and vanilla extract. Using electric mixer at medium speed, beat until cream has thickened. Reduce speed to low and gradually add gelatin. Increase speed to high and beat until cream forms stiff peaks.

8. *Assembly:* Place one shortcake layer in a jar. Cover with 1 tbsp (15 mL) rhubarb compote and spread a thin layer of whipped cream over the compote. Arrange strawberry slices over the top. Spread a second layer of whipped cream over the strawberries. Cover with another layer of sliced strawberries. Place a second circle of cake over the strawberries. Cover with another layer of rhubarb compote. Garnish with remaining whipped cream and a whole strawberry. Repeat until all the jars are filled. Serve immediately or refrigerate for up to 1 hour before serving.

Variation

For the rhubarb compote, replace the orange juice with an equal quantity of passion fruit syrup and cut the sugar in half.

Caribbean Fruit Ricotta Cake

In Italian, the word *ricotta* means "cooked again," because ricotta is made by heating the drained whey of other cooked cheeses. Slightly sweet and mild, ricotta is a natural in desserts. In this recipe it turns Caribbean fruits into a real delight.

Tips

To drain ricotta, wrap it in cheesecloth and leave overnight in the refrigerator, in a colander set over a large bowl.

If you don't have self-rising flour, substitute 1 cup (250 mL) all-purpose flour, 1½ tsp (7 mL) baking powder and ½ tsp (2 mL) salt.

Use fresh pink grapefruit juice, which can be store-bought or freshly squeezed. If you prefer, substitute an equal amount of white grapefruit juice.

- Preheat oven to 350°F (180°C)
- Eight 8-ounce (250 mL) jars, buttered and sprinkled with sugar
- Baking pan large enough to accommodate the jars
- Electric mixer

CAKE

1 cup	butter	250 mL
1¼ cups	granulated sugar	300 mL
3 tbsp	finely grated lemon zest	45 mL
3	large egg yolks	3
1¼ cups	drained ricotta (see Tips, left)	300 mL
3	large egg whites	3
1 cup	self-rising flour (see Tips, left)	250 mL
1 tsp	baking powder	5 mL
½ cup	shredded coconut	125 mL

FRUIT

¾ cup	pink grapefruit juice (see Tips, left)	175 mL
½ cup	cane sugar syrup (see Tip, page 73)	125 mL
¼ tsp	minced chile pepper	1 mL
2	kiwifruit, peeled, halved and sliced	2
1 cup	pineapple chunks	250 mL
1	mango, peeled and diced	1
2	star fruits, sliced	2

1. *Cake:* In a large bowl, using electric mixer at medium speed, beat butter and sugar until light and creamy. Mix in lemon zest, egg yolks and ricotta.

2. In another bowl, using electric mixer with clean beaters at high speed, beat egg whites until they form stiff peaks. Fold into ricotta mixture. Delicately fold in flour, baking powder and coconut.

3. Spoon mixture into prepared jars, dividing equally. Place jars in baking pan, spaced evenly apart and not touching the sides of the pan, and add enough hot water to come halfway up the sides of the jars. Transfer to preheated oven and bake for 25 to 35 minutes or until cakes have risen and are firm and golden.

Tip

Cane sugar syrup is available from organic grocers, fine food shops and some supermarkets. It is made by evaporating the juice from sugarcane plants. It can be replaced by golden syrup or a mixture of equal parts honey and corn syrup (in this recipe, $1/4$ cup/60 mL each).

4. *Fruit:* Meanwhile, in a saucepan over medium heat, combine grapefruit juice, sugar syrup and chile pepper and bring to a boil. Boil for 2 minutes. Remove from heat. Add kiwis, pineapple and mango. Stir to coat fruits with syrup.

5. Remove jars from oven and set aside to cool for 5 minutes. With a spoon, remove a small piece of cake from the center of each. Spoon syrup-coated fruit into center. Garnish each jar with a slice of star fruit and serve warm.

Blueberry and Sour Cream Cake Pudding

Makes 6 servings

Yummy! What else can be said about this treat from the land? Use wild blueberries if possible; they have so much more flavor than the cultivated variety.

Tips

If you don't have self-rising cake flour, substitute 1¾ cups (425 mL) sifted all-purpose flour, ⅓ cup (75 mL) cornstarch, 1 tbsp (15 mL) baking powder and 1 tsp (5 mL) salt. Sift the ingredients twice before using.

Fresh blueberries can be replaced by frozen ones.

You may have leftover batter, depending on the design of the jars. It is important to fill the jars only two-thirds full because the cakes will rise. If you have extra batter, use another jar or bake the batter in a small buttered pan for an extra snack.

- Preheat oven to 350°F (180°C)
- Six 8-ounce (250 mL) jars, buttered
- Electric mixer
- Rimmed baking sheet, lined with parchment paper

2 cups	self-rising cake flour (see Tips, left)	500 mL
1	package (3.5 oz/99 g) vanilla pudding mix	1
1 tsp	baking powder	5 mL
2	egg yolks	2
¾ cup	granulated sugar	175 mL
1½ cups	sour cream	375 mL
3 tbsp	melted salted butter	45 mL
1 tsp	vanilla extract	5 mL
1½ cups	fresh blueberries, divided (see Tips, left)	375 mL
2 tbsp	packed brown sugar	30 mL

1. In a bowl, combine flour, pudding mix and baking powder.

2. In another bowl, using electric mixer at medium speed, beat egg yolks and sugar until pale and fluffy. Beat in sour cream, melted butter and vanilla. Gradually add flour mixture, beating until combined. Fold in half the blueberries.

3. Pour mixture into prepared jars, filling to two-thirds. Top with remaining blueberries. Place jars on baking sheet, spacing evenly apart, and bake in preheated oven for 30 to 40 minutes or until a tester inserted in the centers comes out almost clean.

4. Remove from oven, dust with brown sugar and serve immediately.

Toffee Cake with Caramel Sauce

With its rich, warm flavors, this moist toffee cake — which is closely related to the British classic sticky toffee pudding — is perfect for a cozy night by the fireplace.

Tip

Substitute $\frac{1}{2}$ cup (125 mL) of the water for simmering the dates with $\frac{1}{2}$ cup (125 mL) whisky or cognac.

Make Ahead

The caramel sauce can be prepared one day ahead. Cover and refrigerate. Rewarm over medium heat, stirring constantly.

- Preheat oven to 325°F (160°C)
- Eight 8-ounce (250 mL) jars, buttered
- Electric mixer
- Rimmed baking sheet, lined with parchment paper

CAKE

$\frac{2}{3}$ cup	chopped pitted dates	150 mL
$1\frac{1}{2}$ cups	water, divided	375 mL
2 cups	all-purpose flour	500 mL
1 tsp	baking powder	5 mL
$\frac{1}{4}$ tsp	baking soda	1 mL
1 cup	unsalted butter, at room temperature	250 mL
$\frac{2}{3}$ cup	brown sugar	150 mL
3	large eggs	3
2 tsp	vanilla extract	10 mL

CARAMEL SAUCE

2 cups	heavy or whipping (35%) cream	500 mL
2 cups	packed dark brown sugar	500 mL
$\frac{1}{4}$ cup	corn syrup	60 mL
$\frac{1}{2}$ cup	unsalted butter	125 mL

1. *Cake:* In a saucepan, bring dates and $\frac{3}{4}$ cup (175 mL) water to a boil. Reduce heat and simmer for 6 minutes, stirring, until almost all the liquid has evaporated. Set aside.

2. In a bowl, combine flour, baking powder and baking soda.

3. In a large bowl, using electric mixer at medium speed, beat butter and brown sugar until pale and fluffy. Add eggs one at a time, beating at low speed until each is incorporated. Add vanilla. Add flour mixture and beat at low speed just until incorporated (do not overbeat). Fold in dates. Pour into prepared jars, dividing equally.

4. Place jars on baking sheet, spacing evenly apart, and bake in preheated oven for 30 minutes or until a tester inserted in the centers comes out clean.

5. *Caramel Sauce:* Meanwhile, in a saucepan over medium heat, bring cream, brown sugar, corn syrup and butter to a boil, stirring often. Reduce heat and simmer for 10 minutes. Set aside.

6. Remove jars from oven. Pour half the caramel sauce over the cakes. Return cakes to oven and bake for 8 minutes. Remove from oven and set aside to cool for 10 minutes. Serve with remaining caramel sauce on the side.

Marble Chocolate Cake with Coffee Cream Sauce

Makes 8 servings

This delicious cake is very easy to prepare. Don't be intimidated by the marble part. My first marble cake (made a long time ago) looked more like an almost all chocolate confection, but everybody loved it anyway. The next day I tried again and that effort was perfect! So don't give up.

Tips

Salted butter enhances the taste of the vanilla batter and helps to balance the chocolate. If you are using unsalted butter, add $1/2$ tsp (2 mL) salt to the batter.

Do not overbake the cake. Test it after it has been baking for 30 minutes.

- Preheat oven to 350°F (180°C)
- Eight 8-ounce (250 mL) jars, buttered and sprinkled with sugar
- Rimmed baking sheet, lined with parchment paper

CAKE

2 cups	all-purpose flour	500 mL
1 tbsp	baking powder	15 mL
1 cup	salted butter, softened (see Tips, left)	250 mL
1 cup	sugar, divided	250 mL
$1/2$ tsp	vanilla extract	2 mL
3	large eggs	3
$1/4$ cup	whole milk, divided	60 mL
4 tsp	unsweetened cocoa powder	20 mL

COFFEE CREAM SAUCE

2 cups	heavy or whipping (35%) cream, divided	500 mL
3 tbsp	instant espresso powder, divided	45 mL
3 tbsp	granulated sugar, divided	45 mL

1. *Cake:* Sift flour and baking powder into a bowl and set aside.

2. In a large bowl, beat butter, $3/4$ cup (175 mL) sugar and vanilla until mixture is light and fluffy. Add eggs one at a time, beating well after each addition. Add flour mixture and 2 tbsp (30 mL) milk and beat well.

3. Spoon two-thirds of the mixture into prepared jars, dividing equally.

4. Sift cocoa over remaining third of the mixture and fold in, together with remaining milk and remaining $1/4$ cup (60 mL) sugar. Spoon chocolate mixture over white mixture in jars, dividing equally. Run a skewer through both mixtures, gently swirling them together to create a marbled effect.

Tip

Be certain to follow the instructions when a recipe calls for adding eggs one at a time and mixing well after each addition. If you add the eggs all at once, the mixture might separate.

5. Place jars on baking sheet, spacing evenly apart, and bake in preheated oven for 30 to 40 minutes, until cake comes away slightly from sides of jars and a tester inserted in the center comes out clean (see Tips, page 76). Remove jars from oven and transfer to a wire rack to cool.

6. *Coffee Cream Sauce:* In a bowl, using an electric mixer at medium speed, beat cream and espresso powder until thickened. Slowly add sugar, beating constantly, until soft peaks form.

7. Slice tops off cakes (they will be higher than the jars) and spoon coffee cream over cakes. Return tops to cakes and serve.

Vanilla Cake with Apple Cinnamon Compote

This is real comfort food, the culinary equivalent of putting on a heavy sweater on the first chilly autumn day. Cinnamon is often used with apples for this simple reason: it creates a warm effect in the mouth, comfort in the belly and an unbeatable aroma in the house. What else do we need?

Tips

If you don't have buttermilk, substitute an equal quantity of sour cream.

Because the compote is at the bottom, tapping the jars settles the batter and helps the cake to rise.

- Preheat oven to 350°F (180°C)
- Eight 8-ounce (250 mL) wide-mouth jars, buttered and sprinkled with sugar
- Electric mixer
- Rimmed baking sheet lined with parchment paper

COMPOTE

8	large apples, cored, peeled and diced	8
1 cup	packed brown sugar	250 mL
2 tsp	ground cinnamon	10 mL
¼ cup	unsweetened apple juice	60 mL
1 tsp	finely grated lemon zest	5 mL

CAKE

1¼ cups	all-purpose flour	300 mL
½ tsp	baking powder	2 mL
½ tsp	baking soda	2 mL
Pinch	salt	Pinch
½ cup	unsalted butter, at room temperature	125 mL
1 cup	granulated sugar	250 mL
2	large eggs	2
1	egg yolk	1
½ cup	buttermilk (see Tips, left)	125 mL
2 tsp	vanilla extract	10 mL

1. *Compote:* In a saucepan, combine apples, brown sugar and cinnamon. Add apple juice and bring to a boil, stirring constantly. Reduce heat, add lemon zest and simmer for 15 minutes, stirring often.

2. *Cake:* Meanwhile, in a bowl, combine flour, baking powder, baking soda and salt.

3. In a large bowl, using electric mixer at medium speed, beat butter and sugar until light and fluffy. At low speed, mix in eggs and egg yolk one at a time, beating well after each addition. Add flour mixture, alternating with buttermilk, until just combined. Mix in vanilla.

○

Make Ahead

The apple compote can be prepared up to 2 days ahead and reheated before using.

4. *Assembly:* Spoon 2 tbsp (30 mL) apple compote into each prepared jar. Pour batter over compote, dividing equally. Tap jars gently on counter to even out (see Tips, page 78).

5. Place jars on baking sheet, spacing evenly apart, and bake in preheated oven for 20 minutes or until cake pulls away from sides of jars. Remove from oven, transfer to a wire rack and let cool for 5 minutes.

6. Reheat remaining compote for 3 minutes. Serve cakes with warm apple compote.

Variation

Substitute an equal quantity of pears for the apples. Omit the apple juice and substitute 1 tsp (5 mL) each of nutmeg and cinnamon for the cinnamon.

Pineapple Rum Vanilla Baba

Baba au rhum is a French pastry invented in 1835 in Paris by a descendant of Nicolas Stohrer, pastry chef to Maria of Poland, wife of King Louis XV. Traditional baba dough has to rise slowly overnight to achieve its fine texture, but this quick recipe for baba works really well. True confession: for a long time I thought babas were banal, until I discovered I could dress them up with fruit. My husband loves baba au rhum, so this is a recipe he adores.

Tip

You will need to purchase 2 cans (each 26 oz/796 mL) pineapple chunks in light syrup to have enough syrup for this recipe. Drain off the syrup and set aside. You will have more pineapple than you need. Save the excess for another use, such as adding to fruit salad or to yogurt for quick treat.

- Preheat oven to 425°F (220°C)
- Six 12-ounce (375 mL) jars, buttered
- Electric mixer
- Six medium popover tins (see Tip, page 81) buttered and floured
- Rimmed baking sheet lined with parchment paper

CAKE

3	egg yolks	3
1/2 cup	confectioner's (icing) sugar	125 mL
1 tsp	vanilla extract	5 mL
1/2 cup	all-purpose flour	125 mL
2 tbsp	baking powder	30 mL
1/4 cup	hot milk	60 mL
1/4 cup	melted butter	60 mL
3	egg whites	3
1/2 cup	drained canned pineapple chunks	125 mL

SYRUP

2 cups	syrup from canned pineapple (see Tip, left)	500 mL
1 cup	water	250 mL
1/4 cup	rum	60 mL
1 tsp	vanilla extract	5 mL
1 cup	heavy or whipping (35%) cream	250 mL
3 tbsp	granulated sugar	45 mL
1/2 cup	drained pineapple chunks	125 mL

1. *Cake:* In a bowl, using electric mixer at medium speed, beat egg yolks, confectioner's sugar and vanilla until pale and thick. Beating constantly, add flour, baking powder, milk and butter, beating until smooth.

2. In another bowl, using electric mixer with clean beaters at high speed, beat egg whites to stiff peaks. Delicately fold into yolk mixture. Fold in pineapple chunks.

3. Ladle dough into prepared popover tins. Place tins on prepared baking sheet. Lower oven temperature to 375°F (190°C) and bake for 25 to 35 minutes or until tops are golden brown. Remove from oven and unmold immediately.

I recommend using popover tins because they have enough space for the dough to develop. If you don't have them, use deep muffin tins.

4. *Syrup:* Meanwhile, in a saucepan, combine pineapple syrup, water, rum and vanilla. Bring to a boil over medium heat and boil for 5 minutes. Remove from heat and set aside.

5. *Assembly:* Place one hot baba cake in each jar. Pierce cakes with a toothpick to make tiny holes. Pour warm syrup over cakes, submerging them. Cover jars and set aside for 10 minutes.

6. In a cold bowl, using electric mixer with clean beaters at high speed, whip cream and sugar to stiff peaks. Place about 1 heaping tbsp (20 mL) pineapple chunks in each jar. Top with whipped cream and serve immediately.

Pecan Brittle Mist

Makes 8 servings

This dessert is a family affair. My mother could skip any meal but she never refused a dessert. Pecan cake was one of her many favorites. When I started to bake professionally, I took to partly steaming the cake to give it a spongy texture, and the result was very successful. My mom quickly became a fan, which is a good sign. The brittle recipe comes from my sister.

Tip

Pecans will keep for up to 8 months in the refrigerator and up to 18 months in the freezer. Always refrigerate unused pecans. Since they will absorb odors and flavors, shelled pecans should always be kept in a closed container.

- Preheat oven to 350°F (180°C)
- Eight 8-ounce (250 mL) wide-mouth jars, buttered and sprinkled with sugar
- 2 rimmed baking sheets, lined with parchment paper
- Food processor
- Electric mixer

BRITTLE

2 cups	chopped pecans	500 mL
1½ cups	granulated sugar	375 mL
½ cup	water	125 mL
¼ cup	corn syrup	60 mL
1 tbsp	salted butter	15 mL
½ tsp	baking soda	2 mL

CAKE

2¼ cups	all-purpose flour	560 mL
1 tbsp	baking powder	15 mL
1 tsp	salt	5 mL
1 tsp	ground allspice	5 mL
1¼ cups	salted butter	300 mL
1½ cups	chopped pecans	375 mL
¾ cup	granulated sugar	175 mL
½ cup	packed light brown sugar	125 mL
1 tsp	vanilla extract	5 mL
2	eggs	2

1. *Brittle:* Spread pecans on a prepared baking sheet and roast in preheated oven for 8 minutes. Remove from oven and set aside to cool.

2. In a large saucepan, combine sugar, water, corn syrup and butter. Cook over medium heat, whisking constantly, until mixture turns a medium-dark caramel color. Remove from heat and whisk in baking soda. Pour over roasted pecans. Set pan aside to cool completely.

3. Once it has cooled, break off half of the pecan brittle. Transfer to food processor and pulse until it becomes a coarse powder. Transfer to a bowl and set aside. Set aside leftover brittle for sweet snacks.

Tip

Be certain to follow the instructions when a recipe calls for adding eggs one at a time and mixing well after each addition. If you add the eggs all at once, the mixture might separate.

4. *Cake:* In a large bowl, combine flour, baking powder, salt and allspice.

5. In a saucepan over medium heat, melt butter. Add pecans and cook until butter is lightly browned, stirring constantly. Drain, transferring butter to a measuring cup. Set aside butter and pecans separately.

6. In a large bowl, using electric mixer at medium speed, beat reserved brown butter, granulated and brown sugars and vanilla. Add eggs one at a time, beating after each addition until incorporated. Fold in flour mixture and reserved drained pecans and beat at low speed for 2 minutes, until well incorporated.

7. Pour batter into prepared jars. Place jars on baking sheet and bake in preheated oven for 40 minutes, or until a toothpick comes out clean when inserted in center of cakes. Remove from oven. Place jars on a rack to cool completely. Sprinkle tops of cakes with pecan brittle dust and serve immediately.

Rum-and-Raisin Monkey Bread

Makes 8 servings

Although monkey bread has been around forever and all my friends have fond memories of it, I didn't taste it until a few years ago, at my friend Nicole's house. The fabulous smell of cinnamon permeated the house, and the sticky sauce was just fabulous. No need for a spoon or fork — pull it apart with your fingers and enjoy.

Tips

The jar size may seem large, but the jars will not be filled. If you prefer, serve this dessert in smaller jars with wide openings, dividing the dough and sauce equally.

Depending upon the biscuit dough you use, each roll will produce 6 to 10 biscuits. You will get 24 pieces by cutting 6 biscuits into quarters. If your roll has 10 biscuits, cut each in half to produce 20 pieces and then cut the final 2 pieces in half again to provide the required number.

For a more traditional monkey bread, add 2 tsp (10 mL) ground cinnamon to the sauce in Step 3.

- Preheat oven to 400°F (200°C)
- Eight 16-ounce (500 mL) wide-mouth jars, buttered
- Rimmed baking sheet

1 cup	packed brown sugar	250 mL
2 tbsp	ground cinnamon	30 mL
¾ cup	melted salted butter	175 mL
2	cans (each 12 oz/340 g) biscuit dough	2
¾ cup	raisins	175 mL
1½ cups	spiced rum (see Tips, page 130)	375 mL
2 tbsp	granulated sugar	30 mL

1. In a large bowl, combine brown sugar and cinnamon. Place melted butter in a bowl. Cut each roll of biscuit dough into 24 pieces (see Tips, left). Roll each piece in melted butter and then in the sugar-cinnamon mixture, coating well.

2. Place one piece of prepared dough in the bottom of each prepared jar. Sprinkle with raisins. Continue layering until all biscuit pieces are coated and in the jars, placing raisins between the pieces of dough. Jars should be only half full.

3. In a small saucepan over medium heat, bring spiced rum and sugar to a boil. Boil for 2 minutes. Remove from heat and let cool until warm to the touch. Pour over layered biscuit dough. Cover with plastic wrap and let stand in a warm place for 15 minutes.

4. Transfer jars to baking sheet and place in preheated oven. Lower heat to 350°F (180°C) and bake for 25 to 35 minutes. Remove from oven and let jars cool for 10 minutes before serving.

Banana and Bacon Cake with Strawberry Swirl

Remember the banana-and-strawberry-jam sandwich that was a fixture of school lunches? Who tried it first with bacon? In my family it was my cousin Hugh, who loved anything with bacon. Here is a more sophisticated version: a *"ménage à trois"* made in heaven. This mouth-watering dessert is full of favorite childhood flavors.

Tip

Cook the bacon crisp enough to be crackling but not burnt.

- Preheat oven to 350°F (180°C)
- Electric mixer
- Six 8-ounce (250 mL) wide-mouth jars, greased and floured
- Electric mixer
- Food processor
- Rimmed baking sheet, lined with parchment paper

½ cup	salted butter	125 mL
1 cup	granulated sugar	250 mL
2	eggs	2
1 cup	all-purpose flour	250 mL
1 tsp	baking powder	5 mL
1 tsp	ground cinnamon	5 mL
½ tsp	salt	2 mL
4	bananas, peeled and mashed	4
½ cup	sour cream	125 mL
1	package (3 oz/85 g) strawberry-flavored gelatin	1
8 oz	bacon strips, cooked and crumbled, divided	250 g
2 cups	sliced hulled strawberries	500 mL
1 tbsp	packed brown sugar	15 mL

1. Using electric mixer at medium speed, beat butter and sugar until creamy. Add eggs one at a time, beating well after each addition. Add flour, baking powder, cinnamon and salt and beat until blended. Fold in bananas and sour cream. Transfer half the batter to a medium bowl. Add gelatin and mix well. Add half the bacon pieces to remaining batter.

2. Using two spoons (one for each batter), spoon bacon batter and strawberry batter separately into jars, dividing equally. Using a fork, lightly swirl together, creating a marble effect.

3. Place jars on baking sheet and bake in preheated oven for 35 minutes or until tops are golden. Place on a wire rack and cool completely.

4. In food processor, process strawberries and brown sugar until chopped and blended. Spoon strawberry sauce over cakes, dividing equally. Top with remaining bacon and serve immediately.

Lemon Soufflé

It's a myth that it is difficult to make a soufflé. Try making a soufflé just once and, like all the friends I have similarly convinced, I'm sure you'll agree. The great appeal of a soufflé is its lightness, which leaves space for the taste to develop. And it is perfect after a large meal.

Tips

Use jars with straight sides so the soufflés can rise easily.

To help the soufflés rise, use upward brushstrokes to butter the jars. If you have time, butter the jars, refrigerate them for 30 minutes, then butter again and refrigerate until ready to fill.

Make sure you clean the edges of the jars well before baking.

Use egg yolks from large or extra-large eggs. If using medium-size eggs, add 1 more egg yolk.

Do not open oven to peek while your soufflés are baking — they are likely to collapse.

- Preheat oven to 375°F (190°C)
- Ten 8-ounce (250 mL) wide-mouth straight-sided jars (see Tips, left), buttered and sprinkled with sugar
- Electric mixer
- Fine sieve
- Rimmed baking sheet, lined with parchment paper

8	egg yolks (see Tips, left)	8
3 tbsp	finely grated lemon zest	45 mL
2 tbsp	all-purpose flour	30 mL
¾ cup	granulated sugar, divided	175 mL
1 cup	whole milk	250 mL
¼ cup	unsalted butter, at room temperature	60 mL
¼ cup	freshly squeezed lemon juice	60 mL
10	egg whites, at room temperature	10
	Confectioner's (icing) sugar	

1. In a large bowl, using electric mixer at medium speed, beat egg yolks, lemon zest, flour and 2 tbsp (30 mL) granulated sugar until light and fluffy.

2. In a saucepan over medium heat, bring milk to a boil. Remove from heat and very slowly pour half into the egg yolk mixture, whisking constantly. Whisk in remaining milk. Return mixture to saucepan over low heat and whisk for 4 minutes or until thickened. Strain mixture through sieve placed over a large bowl. Whisk in butter and lemon juice. Set aside.

3. In a bowl, using electric mixer with clean beaters at high speed, beat egg whites until foamy. Gradually add remaining sugar, beating until stiff peaks form. Stir a third of the egg whites into yolk mixture, then, using a rubber spatula, delicately fold in remaining egg whites until just incorporated.

4. Fill each jar to the top and smooth tops with a spatula. With a clean, damp towel, wipe around edges to remove batter from rims.

5. Place jars on baking sheet, spacing apart, and bake in preheated oven for 10 to 15 minutes or until soufflés are golden and puffed up.

6. Remove from oven, dust with confectioner's sugar and serve immediately.

Chocolate and Mint Soufflé

This is a really a faux soufflé, more like a cake-soufflé. We call it "grasshopper cake" because of the green crème de menthe liqueur served with it. It is a fun dessert to prepare for a group of convivial friends.

Tips

For the best results, use jars with straight sides so the soufflés can rise quickly and evenly.

To help the soufflés rise properly, use upward brushstrokes to butter the jars. If you have time, butter the jars, refrigerator them for 30 minutes, then butter again and refrigerate until ready to fill.

Make sure you clean the edges of the jars well before baking.

Use egg yolks from large or extra-large eggs. If using medium-size eggs, add 1 more egg yolk.

Do not open the oven to peek while your soufflés are baking — they are likely to collapse.

- Preheat oven to 350°F (180°C)
- Six 8-ounce (250 mL) wide-mouth straight-sided jars, buttered
- Electric mixer
- Baking pan large enough to accommodate the jars
- Sifter or fine-mesh sieve

4	egg whites	4
Pinch	salt	Pinch
1 cup	granulated sugar, divided	250 mL
½ cup	butter, at room temperature	125 mL
4	egg yolks	4
½ cup	all-purpose flour	125 mL
1½ cups	whole milk	375 mL
2 tsp	mint extract	10 mL
1 cup	grated dark (64%) chocolate	250 mL
¼ cup	green crème de menthe liqueur, optional	60 mL

1. In a large bowl, using electric mixer at high speed, beat egg whites and salt until soft peaks form. Add ¼ cup (60 mL) sugar, 1 tbsp (15 mL) at a time, beating constantly until stiff peaks form.

2. In another large bowl, using electric mixer with clean beaters at medium speed, beat butter and remaining sugar until pale and fluffy. Add egg yolks one at a time, beating well after each addition. Sift flour into the bowl and beat at low speed until incorporated. Add milk and mint extract, beating at low speed. Fold in chocolate.

3. Add beaten egg whites and fold in gently but not completely, leaving a few white streaks.

4. Spoon into jars, filling halfway. Place jars in baking pan, spaced evenly apart and not touching the sides of the pan, and add enough hot water to come halfway up the sides of the jars. Bake in preheated oven for 20 minutes or until a skewer inserted in centers comes out with very moist crumbs adhering.

5. Remove from oven and serve immediately with crème de menthe (if using) on the side, pouring a bit into the soufflé as the first bite is taken.

Variation

Substitute an equal quantity of amaretto for the crème de menthe and almond extract for the mint.

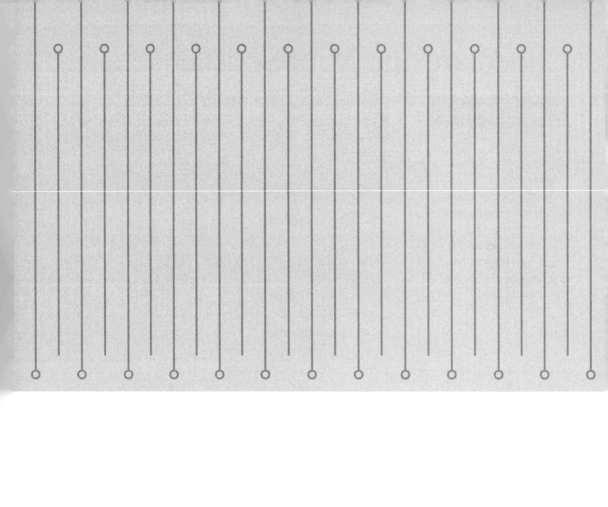

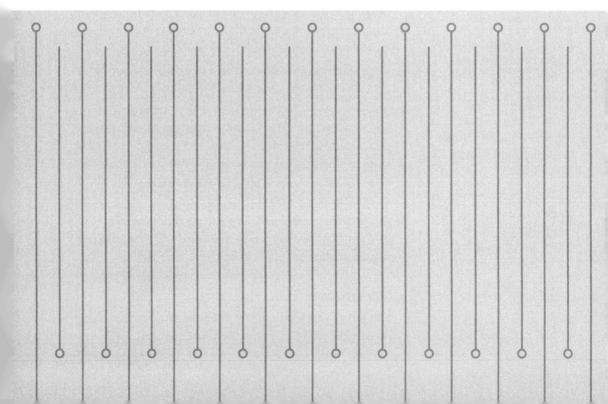

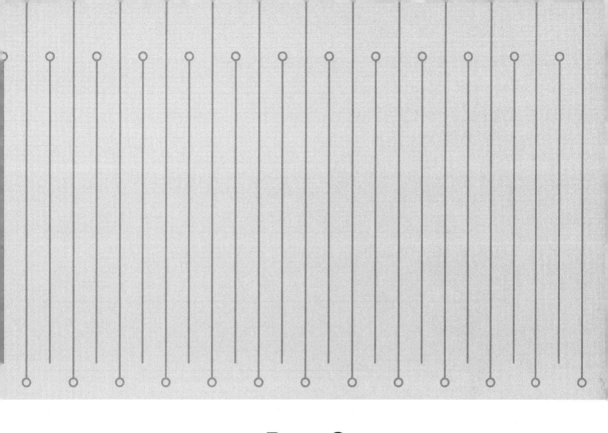

Part 2

From the Fridge

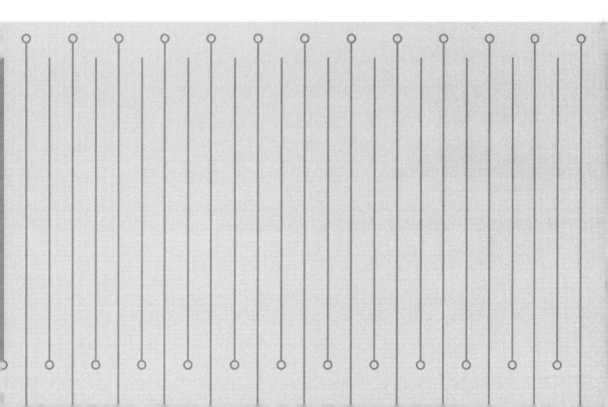

Tutti Frutti

Peach Melba in a Jar

When peaches are paired with raspberries, they can inspire divine dreams. Peach Melba was invented by the famous chef Auguste Escoffier at the end of the 19th century in honor of the Australian diva Nellie Melba. If you prefer, substitute apricots or pears for the peaches.

Tips

Caramelizing the peaches intensifies their taste and makes them particularly luscious.

Choose round, ripe peaches, organically grown if possible. A ripe peach will give very slightly when gently squeezed.

Make Ahead

Freeze the ice cream in the jars a few days ahead of when you plan to serve it.

The peaches can be caramelized a few hours before serving. Keep all the ingredients refrigerated and the final dessert can be assembled in a flash.

- Four 8-ounce (250 mL) jars
- Food processor or blender
- Fine-mesh sieve

4 cups	water	1 L
4	peaches, unpeeled	4
2 tbsp	unsalted butter	30 mL
1½ cups	granulated sugar	375 mL
1	vanilla bean, split lengthwise	1
2 cups	vanilla ice cream	500 mL
¼ cup	heavy or whipping (35%) cream, whipped	60 mL
4 tbsp	slivered almonds	60 mL

RASPBERRY SAUCE

2 cups	raspberries	500 mL
3 tbsp	confectioner's (icing) sugar	45 mL
1 tbsp	freshly squeezed lemon juice	15 mL

1. In a large saucepan, bring water to a boil. Add peaches and return to a boil; reduce heat to medium and poach for 4 minutes. Transfer to a large bowl of cold water and set aside for 5 minutes. Drain and peel off skins. Cut peaches in half and remove stones. Set aside.

2. In a skillet, combine butter, sugar and vanilla bean. Cook over low heat until sugar dissolves. Increase heat to medium and bring to a boil. Add 4 peach halves, cut side down in a single layer, and cook for 3 minutes. Turn peaches over and cook for 3 minutes more. Using a slotted spoon, transfer to a plate and set aside.

3. *Raspberry Sauce:* In food processor fitted with the metal blade (or in a blender), purée raspberries, remaining 4 peach halves, confectioner's sugar and lemon juice, about 4 minutes. Place sieve over a bowl and, using a wooden spoon, press mixture through to remove the seeds. Cover and refrigerate until ready to use.

4. Place a scoop of vanilla ice cream in each jar. Using a spatula, smooth out top of ice cream. Place jars in freezer for at least 10 minutes or up to 2 days.

5. When you are ready to serve, spoon 1 tbsp (15 mL) raspberry sauce on top of ice cream in each jar. Place one peach half on top, cut side up. Fill cavity with raspberry sauce. Garnish with whipped cream and slivered almonds, dividing equally. Serve immediately, with remaining raspberry sauce on the side.

Blackberry Mont Blanc

The original Mont Blanc dessert was so named because it resembles a snow-capped mountain in the Alps. Traditionally it is made with puréed chestnuts topped with whipped cream. For a summer version, blackberries are delightful and elegant.

Tips

When choosing blackberries, make sure they are firm and without blemishes. Blackberries do not keep long in the refrigerator, so use them quickly.

You can use store-bought meringue cookies or make your own (see page 97).

- Four 8-ounce (250 mL) jars
- Food processor
- Electric mixer
- Pastry bag fitted with fluted tip

2 cups	blackberries, divided	500 mL
½ cup	confectioner's (icing) sugar	125 mL
½ tsp	vanilla extract	2 mL
½ tsp	ground ginger	2 mL
1 cup	heavy or whipping (35%) cream	250 mL
8	small meringue cookies (see Tips, left)	8
	Gold candy pearls, optional	

1. Set aside 4 whole blackberries for use as garnish. In food processor fitted with the metal blade, process remaining blackberries, confectioner's sugar, vanilla and ginger for 1 minute.

2. In a large bowl, using electric mixer at high speed, whip cream until soft peaks form. Spoon out 4 tsp (20 mL) whipped cream and set aside in a small bowl. Slowly add blackberry purée to large bowl, beating until stiff peaks form. Transfer to prepared pastry bag.

3. Place some gold candy pearls (if using) in the bottom of each jar. Top with a meringue cookie. Cover with a swirl of blackberry cream. Top with a second meringue. Add 1 tsp (5 mL) whipped cream to each jar and top with a blackberry. Serve immediately.

Soft Meringue with Summer Fruits

This dessert is incredibly easy to make, and it is a spectacular summer treat: sweet, cold, light, fruity and delicious.

Tip

Use homemade or a high-quality store-bought raspberry sorbet. To soften the sorbet, transfer it to the refrigerator for 15 minutes.

- Eight 8-ounce (250 mL) jars
- Food processor
- Electric mixer
- Fine-mesh sieve

1/2 cup	water	125 mL
1 cup	granulated sugar, divided	250 mL
5	peaches, halved and pitted, divided	5
2 cups	fresh raspberries, divided	500 mL
1	cantaloupe, peeled and cut in 1/4-inch (0.5 cm) cubes, divided	1
3 cups	softened raspberry sorbet (see Tip, left)	750 mL
2	large egg whites	2

1. In a saucepan, combine water and 1/2 cup (125 mL) sugar. Bring to a boil over medium heat, stirring constantly, until sugar dissolves. Remove from heat and set aside to cool for 30 minutes.

2. Cut 4 peach halves into 1/4-inch (0.5 cm) cubes and set aside.

3. In food processor fitted with the metal blade, purée remaining peaches, 1 cup (250 mL) raspberries, half of the cantaloupe and 1/4 cup (60 mL) cooled sugar syrup. Pass mixture through a fine-mesh sieve placed over a bowl. Mix in raspberry sorbet. Refrigerate until ready to use.

4. In a bowl, combine cubed peaches and remaining raspberries and cantaloupe. Spoon into jars, dividing equally.

5. Place egg whites in a heatproof bowl and add remaining sugar. Set bowl over a pan of simmering water. Cook, whisking, until sugar dissolves and mixture is hot to the touch and very foamy, about 5 minutes. Remove from heat and, using electric mixer at high speed, beat until stiff, glossy peaks form.

6. Using a spatula, gently fold chilled fruit purée–sorbet mixture into meringue. Spoon into jars over fruit. Freeze for 30 minutes before serving, to chill thoroughly. If you're not serving immediately, transfer to the refrigerator for up to 2 hours.

Frozen Papaya-Meringue Cream

Refreshing is the first word that comes to mind when I think of this recipe — sweet, satisfying and exotic.

Tip
When choosing a papaya, look for yellowish skin and a mushy feel. It's normal for papayas to look bruised.

- Six 8-ounce (250 mL) tall jars
- Electric mixer

1	papaya, halved	1
12	small store-bought meringues	12
2 cups	heavy or whipping (35%) cream	500 mL
1/4 cup	papaya nectar	60 mL
2 tbsp	confectioner's (icing) sugar	30 mL
1 tsp	chopped fresh mint leaves	5 mL
1 cup	vanilla yogurt	250 mL

1. Remove seeds from the papaya and cut flesh into small cubes.

2. Break meringues into small pieces.

3. In a bowl, using electric mixer at medium speed, whisk cream, papaya nectar and sugar until soft peaks form. Fold in papaya, meringue pieces and mint. Delicately fold in yogurt.

4. Pour into jars, dividing equally. Cover with plastic wrap and freeze for at least 4 hours or up to 4 days before serving.

Nectarine Cream with Crunchy Meringue

Makes 4 servings

This is a quick, easy, breezy and simple recipe. You can whip it up in a flash!

Tips

Store-bought meringue cookies are easy to find in a bakery or supermarket. Look for small, airy, crisp white mounds of cooked meringue. If you have homemade meringues, they are even better (see recipe, page 97).

Peach syrup is an intensely flavored liquid that is used for flavoring soda and iced tea, among other things. Look for it in well-stocked supermarkets or specialty stores. Torani, Teisseire and Monin are popular brands. It can be replaced by an equal quantity of peach nectar.

- Four 8-ounce (250 mL) jars
- Blender
- Electric mixer

2 cups	sliced peeled nectarines	500 mL
½ cup	peach syrup (see Tips, left)	125 mL
1 tsp	chopped fresh mint leaves	5 mL
½ cup	sour cream	125 mL
½ cup	heavy or whipping (35%) cream	125 mL
8	small meringue cookies (see Tips, left)	8

1. In a bowl, combine nectarines, peach syrup and mint. Cover and set aside for 15 minutes to blend flavors. Transfer to blender and purée. Add sour cream and blend for 1 minute.

2. In a bowl, using an electric mixer at medium speed, beat cream until soft peaks form. Gradually add nectarine purée and beat until soft peaks form.

3. Crumble meringue cookies and fold into cream. Transfer to jars, dividing equally. Refrigerate for at least 30 minutes or up to 2 hours before serving.

Variation

Peach Cream with Crunchy Meringue: Substitute an equal quantity of peaches for the nectarines.

Apple and Green Peppercorn
Crumble (page 16)

Christmas Pudding (page 28)

Banana Pudding with Salted Caramel Sauce (page 34)

Kiwi and Strawberry Flan (page 48)

Burnt Orange Crème Brûlée (page 59)

Chocolate Gingerbread (page 68)

Strawberry Rhubarb Shortcake (page 70)

Peach Melba in a Jar (page 92)

Blackberry Mont Blanc (page 93)

Tropical Fruit Terrine (page 103)

Lemon Curd and Chocolate Crunch (page 114)

Triple Chocolate Crème (page 119)

Meringue Cookies

**Makes about
5 dozen cookies**

Tips

Use extra meringues
to make sandwich
cookies or serve with
ice cream or fruit
salad, or break them in
small pieces and add to
brownie dough.

Bury your scraped
vanilla pod in
granulated sugar to
make vanilla sugar.

- Preheat oven to 200°F (100°C)
- Electric mixer
- Pastry bag fitted with straight or fancy tip
- Rimmed baking sheet, lined with parchment

3	large egg whites, at room temperature	3
1 cup	granulated sugar	250 mL
1	vanilla pod, split, seeds scraped out and pod discarded	1
Pinch	salt	Pinch
⅛ tsp	cream of tartar	0.5 mL

1. In a heatproof bowl, whisk egg whites, sugar and vanilla seeds until combined.

2. Place bowl over a saucepan half-filled with simmering water. Continue whisking until sugar dissolves completely and mixture is warm and frothy, about 8 minutes. Whisk in salt and cream of tartar.

3. Remove from heat. Using electric mixer at medium speed, beat until mixture is thick, glossy and cool, about 8 minutes.

4. Transfer to prepared pastry bag. Press small mounds of meringue onto prepared baking sheet. Bake in preheated oven for about 2 hours or until cookies are crunchy. Turn off oven and leave cookies in oven for 2 hours (or overnight) to cool completely and dry out. Transfer to an airtight container and store at room temperature in a dry place for up to 2 weeks.

Cardamom-Flavored Frozen Fruit Salad

Years ago, when I lived in Tuscany, the first indication that summer was ending was the branches of my fig trees drooping under the weight of their ripe fruit. Here's a cheerful fruit salad made with luxurious figs, colorful citrus and raspberries. The cardamom adds delicate punch to the honey-sweetened salad.

Tips

Purchase figs that are very tender. Even if they get crushed in the salad, it will still be tasty. Mission figs are terrific.

Figs should be purchased ripe, and only a day or two in advance of when you are planning to eat them. Keep them refrigerated because they go bad quickly.

Make Ahead

This recipe can be made and frozen up to 4 days before you plan to serve it. To achieve a perfect creamy texture, transfer the jars to the refrigerator for 30 minutes before serving.

• Four 8-ounce (250 mL) jars

2 cups	lemon sorbet, softened in the refrigerator for 30 minutes	500 mL
1	ruby red grapefruit, cut into segments (see Tips, page 103)	1
2	navel oranges, cut into segments (see Tips, page 21)	2
1	tangerine, cut into segments	1
5	figs, quartered, divided	5
½ cup	fresh raspberries, divided	125 mL
¼ cup	liquid honey	60 mL
½ cup	freshly squeezed lemon juice	125 mL
1 tbsp	ground cardamom	15 mL
1 tsp	confectioner's (icing) sugar	5 mL

1. In a large bowl, combine citrus segments, 4 of the figs and all but 2 tbsp (30 mL) of the raspberries.

2. In a saucepan, combine juices from the citrus fruits, honey, lemon juice and cardamom. Bring to a boil over medium-high heat. Remove from heat and set aside to cool for 10 minutes.

3. Pour syrup over fruit mixture and gently fold to coat. Add softened sorbet and mix gently. Spoon into jars and place in freezer for at least 2 hours or up to 4 days.

4. To serve, garnish each jar with a few raspberries and one piece of fig. Sprinkle with confectioner's sugar.

Variations

If figs are not available, substitute 8 ounces (250 g) pitted cherries.

Dried figs are available throughout the year. To use them in this recipe, soak them in hot lemon-scented tea for 30 minutes.

Lemony Summer Pudding

A sumptuous pudding, this is a perfect dessert for hot summer nights — or for winter nights when you're wishing it were summer.

Tips

This pudding is traditionally made in the summer, when luscious fresh berries are in abundance. But if fresh berries are not available, an equal quantity of frozen berries can be substituted.

Use larger or smaller jars to make this recipe. Just be sure to divide the contents equally between the jars. If you prefer, recycle used jam or condiment jars to make this recipe.

- Six 8-ounce (250 mL) jars

1½ cups	raspberries	375 mL
1 cup	blueberries	250 mL
3 tbsp	finely grated lemon zest	45 mL
¼ cup	freshly squeezed lemon juice	60 mL
½ cup	granulated sugar	125 mL
Pinch	salt	Pinch
6	thin slices sandwich bread, crusts removed	6
1	lemon, sliced very thinly	1
1 tbsp	confectioner's (icing) sugar	15 mL
	Fresh blueberries and raspberries for garnish, optional	

1. In a saucepan over medium heat, cook raspberries and blueberries, lemon zest and juice for 6 minutes, stirring often. Add sugar and salt; cook, stirring often, for 3 minutes or until sugar is dissolved. Strain berries over a bowl. Reserve berries and syrup separately. Set aside to cool.

2. Using a knife or round cookie cutter, cut bread into 12 circles that will fit into the jars.

3. Pour 1 tbsp (15 mL) reserved berry syrup into each jar and top with 1 bread round. Top with a layer of cooked berries, 1 lemon slice and 1 bread round. Finish with a layer of sauce and berries, topped with a slice of lemon. Using the bottom of a glass, press down firmly. Cover and refrigerate for 3 hours.

4. When you're ready to serve, top with a few fresh berries, if using, and a light dusting of confectioner's sugar.

Ginger and Pear Purée

When winter arrives, I turn to pears to satisfy my yearnings for fruit. Pears have a very delicate flavor, and when paired with the warmth of ginger, they seem to sparkle in the mouth.

Tips

Pear nectar is available in the juice section of supermarkets and natural foods stores.

This recipe calls for store-bought imported gingerbread, a dense, dark brown cake generally available from specialty food shops or supermarkets. It can be replaced by homemade gingerbread.

Prepare extra ground gingerbread and use it for a cheesecake crust or as a topping for ice cream.

This purée can be prepared up to 2 days ahead and refrigerated. You can serve it cold or reheat for 2 minutes in a microwave oven.

I do not recommend freezing this dessert, because it contains brandy.

- Preheat oven to 375°F (190°C)
- Eight 8-ounce (250 mL) jars
- Rimmed baking sheet lined with parchment paper
- Food processor

8	thin slices gingerbread (see Tips, left)	8
12	Anjou pears, peeled, cored and diced	12
1 cup	granulated sugar	250 mL
¼ cup	pear brandy	60 mL
1 cup	pear nectar (see Tips, left)	250 mL
2 tsp	ground ginger	10 mL

1. Place gingerbread on prepared baking sheet. Bake in preheated oven for 5 minutes. Remove from oven and, using a spatula, turn slices over. Return to oven and bake for 10 minutes. Remove from oven and cool completely. Transfer to a food processor and pulse until a fine powder results.

2. In a saucepan, combine pears, sugar, pear brandy and nectar, and ginger. Bring to a boil over medium-high heat. Reduce heat and simmer for 45 minutes or until pears are very tender. Transfer to food processor and purée.

3. Pour pear purée into jars. Top with ground gingerbread and serve immediately, or refrigerate for up to 48 hours and top with gingerbread when ready to serve.

Exotic Fruit Salad with Lemon Balm

Makes 6 servings

If you want a fresh dessert that is full of flavor, this is the recipe. Earl Grey tea, with its crisp bergamot orange flavor, brings a refreshing touch to the fruit salad. Lemon balm, an aromatic member of the mint family, helps to meld the different tastes.

Tips

Other tropical fruits, such as mangos, dates, oranges or — if you can find them — rare purple mangosteens, can be used in this salad.

Look for lemon balm in farmers' markets, fine food shops and even supermarkets. You can also grow your own in small planters; it makes for a beautiful and very fragrant herb. If lemon balm is not available, substitute an equal quantity of mint.

• Six 8-ounce (250 mL) jars

1	Earl Grey teabag	1
1 cup	boiling water	250 mL
3 tbsp	granulated sugar	45 mL
1 cup	freshly squeezed orange juice	250 mL
12	lemon balm leaves (see Tips, left)	12
½	small pineapple, peeled, cored and diced	½
½	papaya, peeled, seeded and diced	½
2	kiwifruit, peeled and diced	2
4	lychees, peeled	4
1	star fruit, sliced	1
1	banana, peeled and sliced	1
2 cups	lemon sorbet, softened in the refrigerator for 15 minutes	500 mL
2 tbsp	chopped lemon balm leaves	30 mL

1. In a cup, combine teabag and boiling water. Set aside to steep for 15 minutes. Remove bag and pour tea into a large bowl. Stir in sugar and orange juice. Add lemon balm leaves and, with the back of a spoon, crush leaves in the liquid. Set aside for 15 minutes to cool.

2. Add pineapple, papaya, kiwis, lychees, star fruit and banana and mix well. Spoon into jars, dividing equally. Cover and refrigerate for 1 hour.

3. Transfer softened sorbet to a bowl. Fold in the chopped lemon balm. Place in freezer for 30 minutes.

4. Place a scoop of sorbet over fruit salad in each jar and serve immediately.

Balsamic-Spiked Strawberry Tartare

A classic tartare is made of beef or fish, plus garnishes, as in steak tartare. This version is a dessert tartare made with strawberries. When I want to impress my friends with a very light dessert, this is often my first choice — especially when I am in a hurry.

Tip

If you can, get the best-quality, oldest balsamic vinegar from either Reggio Emilia (my favorite) or Modena. This will make a big difference to the taste of your tartare. Good balsamic vinegars are actually quite sweet and not very vinegary tasting. They are loaded with complex flavors.

• Four 8-ounce (250 mL) jars

4 cups	hulled strawberries, cut in small cubes	1 L
3 tbsp	confectioner's (icing) sugar	45 mL
3 tbsp	freshly squeezed orange juice	45 mL
2 tsp	finely grated orange zest	10 mL
1 tsp	chopped mint leaves	5 mL
Small pinch	fine sea salt	Small pinch
4 tbsp	balsamic vinegar	60 mL

1. Place cubed strawberries in a large bowl. Sprinkle with confectioner's sugar and toss gently. Add orange juice and mix gently. Cover and set aside for 10 minutes.

2. Drain strawberries, discarding liquid, and return to bowl. Add orange zest, mint and salt and mix very gently. Transfer to jars, dividing equally. Serve immediately or cover and refrigerate for up to 2 hours.

3. When you're ready to serve, top each serving with 1 tbsp (15 mL) balsamic vinegar.

Tropical Fruit Terrine

Makes 6 servings

It always surprises people to learn that the first time I saw a banana I was seven years old. We lived in a remote area where tropical fruits weren't usual (no, I'm not that old!). So when I visited Russia and saw people lining up outside shops in a fierce winter storm to buy "exotic" bananas, I understood their curiosity. While some tropical fruits — such as rambutans, durians, lychees, kumquats, pink bananas and loquats — are still hard to find, this recipe calls for those that are readily available.

Tips

To make grapefruit segments, use a sharp knife to remove the peel and white pith. Holding the fruit over a bowl to catch the juices, cut along each side of the white membranes to remove the segments.

Use jars that are larger or smaller than those called for, to suit what you have available. Just be sure to divide the contents equally.

• Six 8-ounce (250 mL) tall jars

2	packages (each 3 oz/85 g) lime-flavored gelatin	2
3 cups	unsweetened grape juice, divided	750 mL
1 cup	granulated sugar, divided	250 mL
3	kiwifruit, peeled and diced	3
1	large grapefruit, cut into segments, juice reserved (see Tips, left)	1
2	mangos, peeled and diced	2
2	passion fruits	2
2 tbsp	crème fraîche	30 mL

1. In a small bowl, sprinkle gelatin powder over 1 cup (250 mL) grape juice. Set aside to soften for 3 minutes.

2. In a small saucepan over medium-high heat, heat ½ cup (125 mL) sugar with remaining grape juice, whisking until sugar dissolves. Remove from heat and stir in softened gelatin until dissolved. Set aside to cool for 5 minutes.

3. Place a few kiwi slices in bottoms of jars, dividing equally. Add enough gelatin mixture to just cover fruits. Set aside excess gelatin mixture. Refrigerate jars for 2 hours, until gelatin sets.

4. Meanwhile, in a saucepan, combine grapefruit segments and reserved grapefruit juice, mangos and remaining ½ cup (125 mL) sugar. Cook over low heat for 10 minutes, stirring often. Add remaining gelatin mixture and stir gently to dissolve. Remove from heat and set aside until saucepan is cool to the touch.

5. When fruit mixture has cooled, spoon over kiwi layer, dividing equally. Refrigerate for 2 hours or until set.

6. When you're ready to serve, cut passion fruits in half. Using a spoon, remove pulp and seeds. Place the pulp of half a passion fruit in each jar. Serve immediately, topped with a small dollop of crème fraîche.

Variation

Substitute 2 oranges for the grapefruit. Segment and collect the juices as noted in Tips (left).

Grapefruit and Honey Cream

I love grapefruit —
its flavor makes my
mouth water. When
paired with honey, its
acidity disappears and
a wonderful aroma
takes over.

Tips

To segment the
grapefruit for this
recipe, use a sharp knife
to remove the peel and
white pith. Holding
the fruit over a bowl
to catch the juices, cut
along either side of the
white membranes to
remove the segments.
The resulting pure
citrus segments are
often called suprêmes.

When whipping cream,
use a cold bowl for
better results.

If you prefer, substitute
the honey with ¼ cup
(60 mL) granulated
sugar.

- Six 8-ounce (250 mL) jars
- Electric mixer

1	large package (6 oz/170 g) lemon-flavored gelatin	1
1 cup	boiling water	250 mL
1 tbsp	finely grated grapefruit zest	15 mL
2 cups	cold freshly squeezed grapefruit juice	500 mL
3	grapefruit, cut into segments (see Tips, left)	3
1 tsp	chopped lemon balm leaves	5 mL
1 cup	heavy or whipping (35%) cream	250 mL
½ cup	liquid honey	125 mL

1. In a bowl, dissolve gelatin powder in boiling water. Add grapefruit juice and stir well. Add grapefruit segments and lemon balm. Pour into jars, dividing equally. Cover and refrigerate overnight or until set.

2. In a bowl, using electric mixer at high speed, beat cream until thickened. While beating, slowly add honey and beat to soft peaks. Spoon cream into jars, dividing equally. Top with grapefruit zest and serve immediately.

Variation

Orange and Honey Cream: Substitute the grapefruit with oranges. You will need about 5 large navel oranges.

Fig Surprise

I was once challenged by my husband to cook with root beer. *Aha*, he thought, he could catch me there. Quite frankly, I thought so too! But after thinking about the problem I realized that figs and root beer share many subtle flavors. The result was a real surprise for my hubby and a great new addition to my recipe collection.

Tip

Use your favorite brand of root beer — not all of them taste the same.

- Four 8-ounce (250 mL) jars

2 cups	softened vanilla ice cream	500 mL
1/2 cup	unsweetened apple juice	125 mL
1/2 cup	granulated sugar	125 mL
1 cup	root beer	250 mL
1/2 cup	chopped pecans	125 mL
4	large fresh figs	4

1. Place 1 scoop of vanilla ice cream in each jar and freeze for at least 30 minutes or until solid.

2. In a saucepan, combine apple juice and sugar. Bring to a boil over medium heat and cook until sugar dissolves and begins to turn a dark golden color. Remove from heat and set aside for 3 minutes. Standing back, gradually and carefully (it will sputter) stir in root beer. Return to low heat and cook, stirring, for 2 minutes. Remove from heat. Stir in pecans and set aside to cool completely.

3. Cut each fig into quarters. Place 4 quarters in each jar on top of the ice cream. Pour root beer sauce over figs and serve immediately.

Light Pineapple and Star Anise Mousse

The sweet licorice flavor of star anise brings out the unique tangy taste of pineapple. The ricotta cheese mellows this deliciously different dessert.

Tips

For this quantity of pineapple and syrup, purchase a 20-ounce (567 g) can of pineapple chunks. Drain, reserving the syrup and chunks separately.

You need to use canned pineapple juice in this recipe because the bromelain in fresh pineapple keeps gelatin from setting.

- Four 8-ounce (250 mL) jars
- Food processor
- Electric mixer

3	whole star anise	3
1 cup	boiling water, divided	250 mL
½ cup	canned pineapple juice (see Tips, left)	125 mL
1 cup	pineapple chunks (see Tips, left)	250 mL
1 cup	pineapple syrup (see Tips, left)	250 mL
2 tbsp	unflavored gelatin powder	30 mL
2 tsp	finely grated orange zest	10 mL
1 cup	ricotta cheese	250 mL
½ cup	light sour cream	125 mL
1 cup	confectioner's (icing) sugar, divided	250 mL
1 cup	heavy or whipping (35%) cream	250 mL
3 tbsp	chopped cashews	45 mL
1 tsp	ground star anise (see Tip, page 107)	5 mL

1. In a saucepan, combine star anise, ½ cup (125 mL) boiling water and pineapple juice. Bring to a boil, reduce heat and simmer for 5 minutes. Remove from heat. Remove and discard star anise. Set syrup aside.

2. In food processor fitted with the metal blade, purée pineapple chunks. Set aside.

3. Pour pineapple syrup into a bowl. Sprinkle with gelatin powder. Set aside for 5 minutes. Pour remaining boiling water over gelatin and stir until smooth. Stir in orange zest and reserved star anise syrup.

4. Using electric mixer at medium speed, beat ricotta until smooth, about 4 minutes. Beat in sour cream and ¾ cup (175 mL) confectioner's sugar, until silky. Reduce speed to low and beat in gelatin mixture. Fold in pineapple purée.

Tip

To grind star anise, use a clean electric coffee grinder (preferably one reserved specifically for grinding spices) or a mortar and pestle (if you have the strength and patience) to pulverize it into a fine powder. Or look for star anise that is already ground.

5. In a clean bowl, using electric mixer with clean beaters at high speed, beat heavy cream with remaining confectioner's sugar until stiff peaks form. Gently fold into ricotta mixture. Pour into jars, dividing equally. Using a spatula, gently smooth tops. Refrigerate overnight or for up to 48 hours.

6. In a bowl, combine cashews and ground star anise. When you are ready to serve, sprinkle each jar with mixture, dividing equally. Serve immediately.

Grilled Banana and Whisky Mousse

This is definitely a grown-up dessert, one that would be perfect after a long day of skiing or a brisk walk in the forest.

Tips

For best results, use bananas that are not too ripe.

I prefer to use smoky Scotch whisky because of its very characteristic flavor that stays on the palate, but you can use Canadian (rye) whiskey, American bourbon or any other whisky you have on hand.

Look for dried banana chips in the fresh fruit department of supermarkets or at organic fine food shops. They are often available in mixed dried fruit packages.

- Preheat oven to 400°F (200°C)
- Preheat broiler
- Six 8-ounce (250 mL) jars
- Rimmed baking sheet, lined with parchment paper
- Food processor
- Electric mixer

4	bananas, peeled and sliced	4
2 tbsp	packed brown sugar	30 mL
3½ oz	milk chocolate, chopped	100 g
2 tbsp	butter	30 mL
¼ cup	freshly brewed strong coffee	60 mL
¼ cup	whisky (see Tips, left)	60 mL
2	large egg yolks	2
¼ cup	granulated sugar, divided	60 mL
3 tbsp	water	45 mL
2	large egg whites	2
Pinch	salt	Pinch
2 tbsp	confectioner's (icing) sugar	30 mL
¾ cup	heavy or whipping (35%) cream	175 mL
	Dried banana chips for garnish (see Tips, left)	

1. Place banana slices on prepared baking sheet. Sprinkle with brown sugar. Place under preheated broiler for 4 minutes or until well caramelized. Remove from oven and set aside to cool for 10 minutes. Transfer to food processor fitted with the metal blade and purée.

2. In a saucepan, combine chopped chocolate, butter and coffee. Bring to a simmer over low heat, whisking constantly, until chocolate is completely melted. Remove from heat and stir in whisky.

3. In a large bowl, using electric mixer at medium speed, beat egg yolks and 2 tbsp (30 mL) granulated sugar until pale and thick.

Tip

Use larger or smaller jars to make this recipe. Just be sure to divide the contents equally between the jars. If you prefer, recycle used jam or condiment jars to make this recipe.

4. In a small saucepan, combine remaining granulated sugar and water. Bring to a boil, stirring, until sugar dissolves. Beating constantly, pour mixture into egg yolks. Add chocolate mixture and beat for 2 minutes. Fold in banana purée.

5. In a clean bowl, using electric mixer with clean beaters at high speed, beat egg whites with salt until stiff peaks form. Gradually beat in confectioner's sugar. Fold gently into chocolate mixture.

6. In another clean bowl, using electric mixer with clean beaters at high speed, beat heavy cream until soft peaks form. Fold into chocolate mixture.

7. Pour into jars, dividing equally. Refrigerate for at least 2 hours or up to 2 days. When you are ready to serve, garnish with dried banana chips.

Blueberry Cream Cheese Mousse

Light and creamy but refreshing, this mousse is a wonderful summer treat. Cream cheese sharpens the unique taste of blueberries and makes this dessert unforgettable.

Tips

Always choose fresh blueberries that have not been crushed.

Always bring cream cheese to room temperature before using.

- Four 8-ounce (250 mL) jars
- Electric mixer

2 tbsp	hot water	30 mL
1 tbsp	unflavored gelatin powder	15 mL
2 cups	fresh blueberries, divided	500 mL
2 tbsp	granulated sugar	30 mL
4	egg whites	4
1½ cups	cream cheese, at room temperature (see Tips)	375 mL
1 cup	vanilla yogurt	250 mL
½ tsp	vanilla extract	2 mL
1 tbsp	confectioner's (icing) sugar	15 mL

1. Pour hot water into a small bowl. Sprinkle with gelatin and set aside for 5 minutes.

2. In a saucepan, combine 1½ cups (375 mL) blueberries and granulated sugar. Cook over low heat for 15 minutes, stirring often. Add gelatin mixture and whisk to incorporate. Set aside to cool.

3. Meanwhile, in a bowl, using electric mixer at high speed, beat egg whites to stiff peaks.

4. In a large bowl, combine cream cheese, yogurt and vanilla, beating to combine. Fold beaten egg whites into mixture until just combined. Transfer half to a separate bowl. Add cooled blueberry mixture and mix well.

5. Spoon a layer of the plain mixture into jars, dividing equally. Add a layer of the blueberry mixture, dividing equally. Cover and refrigerate for at least 2 hours or up to 6 hours before serving.

6. To serve, top with remaining blueberries and sprinkle with confectioner's sugar.

Banana Mousse with Cardamom and Chocolate Sauce

Banana mousse is one of the first desserts I made, and as far as I can remember, everyone loved it. Through the years I've discovered that spices, particularly cardamom, pair very well with bananas. As for chocolate sauce — well, that's just a must.

Tip

For best results, use bananas that are ripe but not yet black.

- Six 8-ounce (250 mL) jars
- Blender
- Electric mixer

2 cups	chocolate sauce, divided	500 mL

BANANA MOUSSE

3	ripe bananas	3
2 tbsp	packed brown sugar	30 mL
1½ tsp	ground cardamom	7 mL
1 cup	heavy or whipping (35%) cream	250 mL
3 tbsp	confectioner's (icing) sugar, divided	45 mL
3	egg whites	3

1. Pour 1 cup (250 mL) chocolate sauce into jars, dividing equally. Set aside in refrigerator, along with remaining chocolate sauce.

2. *Banana Mousse:* In blender, purée bananas, brown sugar and cardamom.

3. In a bowl, using electric mixer at high speed, beat cream and 2 tbsp (30 mL) confectioner's sugar until stiff peaks form. Delicately fold in banana purée.

4. In another bowl, using electric mixer with clean beaters at high speed, beat egg whites and remaining confectioner's sugar until stiff peaks form. Fold into banana cream.

5. *Assembly:* Spoon banana mousse into jars on top of chocolate sauce and refrigerate for 2 hours. When you're ready to serve, drizzle remaining chocolate sauce over the top and serve immediately.

Deliciously Creamy

Lemon Curd and Chocolate Crunch

Makes 6 servings

What would life be without a little zest — of lemon, of course. Sharp and subtle, cooling and pleasant, the satin texture of lemon curd complements the rich chocolaty crunch in this yummy recipe. Think about making a double quantity; you'll want extra to give your guests to take home.

Tip

When using egg yolks, pass them through a fine-mesh strainer to avoid lumps. The final texture will benefit from that extra attention.

Make Ahead

The lemon curd can be made and refrigerated up to 2 days in advance. If making the lemon curd in advance, cover it with plastic wrap pressed directly onto the surface, to prevent a skin from forming.

- Six 8-ounce (250 mL) wide-mouth jars
- Rimmed baking sheet, lined with parchment paper
- Fine-mesh sieve

CHOCOLATE CRUNCH

7 oz	dark chocolate, coarsely chopped	210 g
2 cups	crisped rice cereal	500 mL

LEMON CURD

7	large egg yolks (see Tip, left)	7
1½ cups	granulated sugar	375 mL
2 tbsp	finely grated lemon zest	30 mL
¾ cup	freshly squeezed lemon juice	175 mL
⅛ tsp	kosher or coarse sea salt	0.5 mL
½ cup	cold unsalted butter, cut into small pieces	125 mL
	Cold water	
	Ice cubes	

GARNISH

2 tbsp	unsweetened cocoa powder	30 mL
2 tbsp	granulated sugar	30 mL

1. *Chocolate Crunch:* Place chocolate in a large, microwave-safe bowl. Cover and microwave on High for 1 minute. Stir well, until evenly melted. Gradually add cereal, folding in gently, until completely coated.

2. Transfer to prepared baking sheet, spreading evenly. Place in freezer for 45 minutes, until solid. Remove from freezer and, with a thick knife, chop into tiny pieces. Refrigerate until ready to use.

3. *Lemon Curd:* Meanwhile, make the curd. Pass egg yolks through sieve into a saucepan. Whisk in sugar, lemon zest and juice and salt. Cook over medium heat, stirring constantly with a wooden spoon, until mixture has thickened and coats the back of the spoon, about 10 minutes. Remove from heat. Add butter and stir until melted. Strain through sieve into a bowl. Set bowl over a large bowl of ice water. Whisk for 5 minutes to cool.

Tip

Use larger or smaller jars to make this recipe. Just be sure to divide the contents equally between the jars. If you prefer, recycle used jam or condiment jars to make this recipe.

4. *Assembly*: Pour one-third of the lemon curd into jars, dividing equally. Add half of the chocolate crunch, dividing equally. Add half of the remaining lemon curd and cover with remaining chocolate crunch. Top with remaining lemon curd. Cover loosely with plastic and refrigerate for at least 2 hours or up to 2 days.

5. *Garnish*: In a bowl, mix cocoa powder and granulated sugar. Sprinkle evenly over top of each jar and serve immediately.

Variation

Orange Curd and Chocolate Crunch: Substitute equal quantities of orange zest and juice for the lemon.

Banana Cream Pie Crunch

Bananas are easy to find all year round, they're easy to cook with and everyone loves them. This moist dessert is immensely satisfying.

Tips

Don't peel and slice the bananas until you are ready to use them; otherwise they will turn brown.

For extra crunchiness, you can double the coconut-crumb mixture and place half at the bottom of the jars before filling.

Make Ahead

This dessert can be made one day ahead and kept refrigerated.

- Eight 8-ounce (250 mL) jars
- Food processor
- Electric mixer
- Fine-mesh sieve

BANANA CREAM

¾ cup	granulated sugar	175 mL
⅓ cup	all-purpose flour	75 mL
2 tbsp	cornstarch	30 mL
Pinch	salt	Pinch
3 cups	whole milk	750 mL
4	egg yolks	4
1 tsp	vanilla extract	5 mL
¼ cup	cold unsalted butter, diced	60 mL
2	bananas, peeled and sliced	2

TOPPING

½ cup	graham cracker crumbs	125 mL
3 tbsp	coconut flakes	45 mL
2 tbsp	butter	30 mL
1 tbsp	packed brown sugar	15 mL
2	bananas, peeled and sliced	2

1. *Banana Cream:* In food processor fitted with the metal blade, process sugar, flour, cornstarch and salt for 1 minute. Transfer to a large saucepan. Gradually whisk in milk. Warm over medium heat for 2 minutes (do not boil).

2. In a bowl, using electric mixer at medium speed, beat egg yolks until thick. Gradually add warm milk mixture, beating constantly. Add vanilla. Transfer to saucepan and cook over medium heat, stirring constantly, until mixture comes to a boil and thickens. Remove from heat and whisk in butter. Set aside.

3. In food processor, purée bananas. Press purée through sieve and fold into cream. Pour into jars, dividing equally. Press plastic wrap directly onto the surface and refrigerate for at least 6 hours or up to 24 hours.

4. *Topping:* In food processor, pulse crumbs and coconut flakes until combined. Set aside.

5. In a skillet, melt butter and brown sugar. Add banana slices and cook over high heat just enough to caramelize lightly. Place on top of chilled banana cream, dividing equally. Top with reserved coconut-crumb mixture and serve immediately.

Praline and Papaya Crunch

With its rich pinkish orange flesh, papaya is a very popular tropical fruit. I like to add a bit of black pepper to papaya — it echoes the peppery flavor of its seeds.

Tips

You will have extra praline powder, but it will keep for up to 2 weeks in a jar. Use it to top ice cream or mix into cereals and yogurt.

To dice the papaya, cut it in half and spoon out the seeds. Set aside 2 tbsp (30 mL) seeds to use as garnish. Score the flesh, then scoop out and dice.

If almond-flavored yogurt is not available, substitute an equal quantity of vanilla yogurt.

- Four 10-ounce (300 mL) jars
- Rimmed baking sheet lined with buttered parchment paper
- Food processor

PRALINE

1 cup	pecans, coarsely chopped	250 mL
1 cup	chopped almonds	250 mL
2 cups	granulated sugar	500 mL
3 tbsp	butter	45 mL
1 tsp	vanilla extract	5 mL

PAPAYA

1	papaya, seeds reserved, diced (½ inch/1 cm; see Tips, left)	1
2 tbsp	freshly squeezed lime juice	30 mL
¼ tsp	freshly ground black pepper	1 mL
2 cups	almond-flavored yogurt, divided (see Tips, left) plus additional for garnishing	500 mL

1. *Praline:* Spread pecans and almonds on prepared baking sheet in a single layer.

2. In a large skillet, cook sugar over medium heat, shaking the pan occasionally, until it begins to melt. Reduce heat to low and cook until golden brown. Remove from heat. Standing well back, add butter and vanilla, stirring until all is melted and incorporated. Pour over nuts, spreading evenly.

3. Using a fork and working quickly, roll nuts in caramel. Set aside to cool completely. When cool, break into small clusters. Transfer to food processor and pulse to chop finely.

4. *Papaya:* In a bowl, combine papaya, lime juice and pepper. Mix well and set aside.

5. *Assembly:* Spoon 1 cup (250 mL) yogurt into jars, dividing equally. Cover with 1 tbsp (15 mL) praline powder per serving and half of the diced papaya, dividing equally. Repeat. Top each jar with a dollop of yogurt. Garnish with papaya seeds, dividing equally, and serve immediately.

Chocolate and Coffee Petite Crème

In this classic French dessert, chocolate and coffee team up for a truly sinful delight. I love this flavor combination, but it is on the rich side, so serve it in small portions.

Tip

Using the best-quality chocolate is always important because its high content of cocoa butter brings a more complex and finer taste to desserts. (Lower-grade chocolate substitutes vegetable oils for cocoa butter.) In this recipe, good chocolate brings a rich flavor that will not dissipate.

Make Ahead

This crème can be prepared up to 48 hours in advance, covered and refrigerated.

- Preheat oven to 325°F (160°C)
- Eight 4-ounce (125 mL) jars
- Fine-mesh sieve
- Baking pan large enough to accommodate the jars
- Electric mixer

1 cup	finely chopped dark (64%) chocolate	250 mL
3 cups	heavy or whipping (35%) cream, divided	750 mL
2 tbsp	instant espresso powder	30 mL
4	large egg yolks	4
4 tbsp	granulated sugar, divided	60 mL
1/2 tsp	vanilla extract	2 mL
Pinch	salt	Pinch
1 tsp	cornstarch	5 mL

1. Place chopped chocolate in a bowl.

2. In a saucepan, bring 2 cups (500 mL) cream and espresso powder to a simmer. Pour over chocolate. Stir gently until chocolate is melted. Set aside for 5 minutes.

3. In a large bowl, whisk together egg yolks, 2 tbsp (30 mL) sugar, vanilla and salt. Whisk in reserved chocolate mixture and cornstarch. Pour through sieve into a large bowl.

4. Place jars in baking pan, spaced evenly apart and not touching the sides of the pan, and add chocolate mixture, dividing equally. Add enough hot water to come halfway up the sides of the jars. Cover pan with aluminum foil and bake in preheated oven for 25 minutes or until custards are just set and still wobbly.

5. Remove from oven and transfer jars to a wire rack. Cool for 15 minutes, then cover and refrigerate for at least 3 hours or up to 48 hours.

6. In a large bowl, using electric mixer at high speed, beat remaining cream and sugar until stiff peaks form. Place a spoonful of whipped cream on each chocolate crème and serve immediately.

Triple Chocolate Crème

My dad was a pastry chef, and a terrific one to boot. So I grew up surrounded by sugar flowers, rivers of caramel and chocolate extravaganzas. To his great despair, I did not really like chocolate, but my attitude changed on a trip to Europe, when I tasted an ice cream that woke up my palate. Good chocolate is expensive but it takes just a little to satisfy you, so always choose the best quality.

Tip

If you want your parfaits to be absolutely perfect, place the softened ice cream, chocolate pudding and white chocolate cream in three separate pastry bags, piping the ingredients into the jars as indicated in Step 5. That way you can fill the jars while leaving the sides clean. Then freeze briefly (for 10 to 20 minutes) before serving.

If you are serving this to adults, pour a bit of chocolate or coffee liqueur between the ice cream and pudding layers to enhance the flavors.

- Eight 8-ounce (250 mL) jars
- Electric mixer

CHOCOLATE PUDDING

1 cup	granulated sugar	250 mL
1 cup	unsweetened cocoa powder	250 mL
1/4 cup	cornstarch	60 mL
Pinch	salt	Pinch
2 1/2 cups	milk	625 mL
4	large egg yolks	4
2 tbsp	cold unsalted butter, in pieces	30 mL
1/2 tsp	vanilla extract	2 mL

WHITE CHOCOLATE CREAM

2 cups	heavy or whipping (35%) cream	500 mL
2 tbsp	confectioner's (icing) sugar	30 mL
1/2 cup	white chocolate shavings	125 mL
2 cups	softened chocolate ice cream	500 mL
2 tbsp	grated milk chocolate	30 mL

1. *Chocolate Pudding:* In a saucepan, whisk together sugar, cocoa, cornstarch and salt. Very slowly add milk, whisking constantly, and whisk until cornstarch is completely absorbed. Whisk in egg yolks one at a time.

2. Cook over medium heat, whisking constantly, until mixture starts to boil. Reduce heat to low and cook for 1 minute. Remove from heat and transfer to a bowl. Mix in butter and vanilla.

3. Cover with plastic wrap placed directly on surface of pudding (to prevent a skin from forming) and chill for at least 4 hours or up to 2 days. Before using, whisk pudding until smooth.

4. *White Chocolate Cream:* In a large bowl, using electric mixer at medium speed, beat heavy cream and confectioner's sugar until soft peaks form. Add white chocolate and beat until stiff peaks form.

5. *Assembly:* Place a layer of chocolate ice cream at the bottom of each jar, dividing equally. Top with a thick layer of chocolate pudding, dividing equally. Cover with a layer of white chocolate cream, dividing equally. Top with grated milk chocolate, dividing equally. Serve immediately.

Chocolate Cream Pie

Makes 6 servings

Rich is the first word that comes to mind when I imagine chocolate cream pie. It also needs to be silky and full of flavor. In a jar, the fun part is placing the "crust" in the center, so every bite contains a bit of chocolaty crispness.

Tips

The chocolate cream can be prepared and refrigerated for up to 2 days before serving.

Choose good-quality chocolate. It will make a big difference in the end result.

- Six 8-ounce (250 mL) jars
- Electric mixer
- Food processor

CHOCOLATE CUSTARD

½ cup	granulated sugar	125 mL
⅓ cup	unsweetened cocoa powder	75 mL
¼ cup	cornstarch	60 mL
½ tsp	salt	2 mL
2 cups	whole milk	500 mL
1 cup	half-and-half (10%) cream	250 mL
½ cup	finely chopped bittersweet (64% or 70%) chocolate	125 mL
4	large egg yolks	4
1 tsp	vanilla extract	5 mL
24	chocolate wafer cookies	24

TOPPING

½ cup	heavy or whipping (35%) cream	125 mL
1 tbsp	confectioner's (icing) sugar	15 mL
¼ cup	finely grated chocolate	60 mL

1. *Chocolate Custard:* In a small bowl, whisk together sugar, cocoa, cornstarch and salt. Set aside.

2. In a saucepan, combine milk, half-and-half and chocolate. Stir over medium heat until chocolate melts. Remove pan from heat.

3. Pour 1 cup (250 mL) hot chocolate mixture into sugar mixture and whisk until smooth. Add to mixture in saucepan and whisk until incorporated. Return to stovetop and cook over medium heat, stirring constantly, for about 6 minutes, until bubbly and thick.

4. In a large bowl, using electric mixer at medium speed, beat egg yolks until pale. Add milk mixture in a slow, steady stream, beating constantly. Return to saucepan and cook over low heat, stirring constantly, for 4 minutes or just until mixture begins to boil. Remove from heat and stir in vanilla. Place saucepan on a wire rack and set aside to cool for 15 minutes, whisking often.

Use larger or smaller jars to make this recipe. Just be sure to divide the contents equally between the jars. If you prefer, recycle used jam or condiment jars to make this recipe.

5. In food processor, pulse cookies into fine crumbs.

6. Spoon chocolate custard into jars, filling to halfway. Cover with a thin layer of cookie crumbs. Fill jars with remaining custard. Place plastic wrap directly on surface of custards. Refrigerate for at least 4 hours or up to 2 days.

7. *Topping:* In a cold bowl, using electric mixer at high speed, whip heavy cream and confectioner's sugar to stiff peaks. Fold in grated chocolate. Garnish each jar with a dollop of whipped cream and serve immediately.

Choco Mint Mousse

Velvety and pleasantly refreshing, this dessert offers the richness of chocolate and a burst of freshness from the mint. It truly is spectacular on the tongue. This dessert is designed for a crowd and must be made the day before you intend to serve it. It's a natural for get-togethers that will benefit from a strong statement for dessert.

Tip

Use larger or smaller jars to make this recipe. Just be sure to divide the contents equally between the jars. If you prefer, recycle used jam or condiment jars to make this recipe.

- Eight 8-ounce (250 mL) jars
- Electric mixer

3¼ cups	heavy or whipping (35%) cream, divided	800 mL
1 cup	grated white chocolate	250 mL
1 tsp	mint extract	5 mL
¾ cup	confectioner's (icing) sugar, divided	175 mL
3 tbsp	green crème de menthe	45 mL
½ cup	grated dark (70%) chocolate	125 mL
1½ cups	grated semisweet (55%) chocolate	375 mL
¼ cup	2% milk	60 mL
12	fresh mint leaves, chopped	12
	Mint leaves for garnish	

1. In a saucepan, combine 1 cup (250 mL) cream and white chocolate. Cook, stirring, over low heat until chocolate is melted and mixture is smooth. Stir in mint extract. Remove from heat and set aside to cool.

2. In a bowl, using electric mixer at high speed, beat 1 cup (250 mL) cream and half of confectioner's sugar until stiff peaks form. Beat in crème de menthe. Gently fold in cooled white chocolate mixture. Very delicately fold in dark chocolate. Transfer to jars, dividing equally. Cover and refrigerate for at least 1 hour or up to 4 hours.

3. In a large, heatproof bowl set over a saucepan of simmering water (but not touching the water), combine semisweet chocolate and milk. Cook, stirring, until melted and well combined. Remove from heat and set aside to cool, about 10 minutes.

4. In a bowl, using electric mixer at medium speed, beat remaining cream and confectioner's sugar until mixture just starts to thicken. Whisk in melted semisweet chocolate mixture, whisking until stiff peaks form. Add chopped mint and whisk just until combined.

5. Carefully spoon (or use a pastry bag fitted with a decorating tip) semisweet chocolate mousse into jars, dividing equally. Refrigerate for at least 30 minutes or for up to 4 hours. Serve chilled, garnished with mint leaves.

Apricot and Chocolate Chip Pudding with Quinoa

I was looking for something different to do with apricot pudding when the chocolate chips in my pantry called for my attention. They desperately wanted to be part of this pudding, and boy, were they right, because this is absolutely divine.

Tip

Quinoa, which has a pleasantly nuanced nutty flavor, is available in most supermarkets and natural foods stores.

- Eight 8-ounce (250 mL) jars
- Food processor
- Electric mixer

1 cup	chopped dried apricots, divided	250 mL
	Boiling water	
2 cups	milk, divided	500 mL
2 cups	half-and-half (10%) cream, divided	500 mL
½ cup	quinoa	125 mL
2	eggs	2
½ cup	granulated sugar	125 mL
¼ tsp	ground cardamom	1 mL
¼ tsp	ground nutmeg	1 mL
½ cup	chocolate chips	125 mL
	Plain or vanilla yogurt, optional	

1. Place half the dried apricots in a bowl and cover with boiling water. Set aside for 30 minutes.

2. Using a slotted spoon, transfer soaked apricots to food processor, fitted with the metal blade, and purée.

3. In a large saucepan, combine 1 cup (250 mL) milk and 1 cup (250 mL) half-and-half. Add quinoa and bring to boil, stirring. Reduce heat to low and simmer for 15 minutes, stirring often.

4. In a large bowl, using electric mixer at medium speed, beat eggs and sugar until pale and thick. Add cardamom, nutmeg and remaining milk and half-and-half.

5. Add to quinoa and cook over low heat, stirring constantly, for 5 minutes. Add apricot purée and mix well. Fold in remaining apricots and cook, stirring constantly, for 5 minutes. Remove from heat and transfer to a bowl. Set aside to cool for 5 minutes. Fold in chocolate chips. Transfer to jars, dividing equally. Cover with plastic wrap placed directly on surface of puddings and refrigerate overnight or for up to 2 days. Serve cold, topped with a dollop of yogurt, if using.

Milk Chocolate Cream with Passion Fruit Coulis

The first time I saw a passion fruit, I was in Africa, where this small and rather ugly fruit seemed to grow everywhere. When you smell it, taking in all its fragrant energy, you realize the possibilities. And when you taste it, its tart, citrusy flavor calls on all your senses. Paired with the silkiness of milk chocolate, passion fruit finds its way straight to my heart.

Tips

To prepare the passion fruit, cut in half; scoop out the pulp and seeds.

This recipe for chocolate cream contains no egg.

Substitute half-and-half (10%) cream for the light cream for a richer pudding.

If you have an espresso machine, use it to foam the milk as if making cappuccino.

Make chocolate shavings by passing a potato peeler over the narrow edge of a cold chocolate bar or block of chocolate. Keep shavings refrigerated in a covered container.

- Six 8-ounce (250 mL) jars
- Immersion blender

CHOCOLATE CREAM

1/4 cup	granulated sugar	60 mL
1 tbsp	packed brown sugar	15 mL
3 tbsp	cornstarch	45 mL
3 cups	light (5%) cream, divided (see Tips, left)	750 mL
1/2 tsp	vanilla extract	2 mL
12 oz	milk chocolate, chopped	375 g

PASSION FRUIT COULIS

4	passion fruit (pulp and seeds)	4
3 tbsp	confectioner's (icing) sugar	45 mL
2 tbsp	freshly squeezed lemon juice	30 mL

TOPPING

1/2 cup	whole milk	125 mL
1 tbsp	chocolate shavings (see Tips, left)	15 mL

1. *Chocolate Cream:* In a bowl, mix granulated and brown sugars, cornstarch, 1/4 cup (60 mL) cream and vanilla. Set aside.

2. In a saucepan, bring remaining cream to a boil. Remove from heat, add chopped chocolate and stir well. Add cornstarch mixture and bring to a boil, whisking constantly. Boil for 2 minutes, until thickened. Remove from heat and transfer to jars, dividing equally. Refrigerate for 4 hours.

3. *Passion Fruit Coulis:* In a saucepan, mix passion fruit, confectioner's sugar and lemon juice. Over medium heat, bring to a boil, stirring constantly. Lower heat and simmer until syrup has thickened. Set aside to cool for 10 minutes. Pour over chilled chocolate cream, dividing equally, and refrigerate for 1 hour.

4. *Topping:* In a saucepan, heat milk until bubbles appear around the edge (do not boil). Using an immersion blender (see Tips, left), whisk until thick foam forms on top. Place 1 tbsp (15 mL) milk foam on top of each dessert. Top with chocolate shavings and serve immediately.

Peanut Butter and Chocolate Cup

Peanut butter and chocolate is probably the best-known flavor match in North America. I can say unequivocally that this is my daughter's favorite dessert. The salty peanuts and chocolate are just made for each other.

Tips

Using the best-quality chocolate will make a big difference in the end product.

Use larger or smaller jars to make this recipe. Just be sure to divide the contents equally between the jars. If you prefer, recycle used jam or condiment jars to make this recipe.

- Four 8-ounce (250 mL) jars
- Electric mixer
- Pastry bag fitted with straight tip

CHOCOLATE LAYER

8 oz	chopped milk chocolate	250 g
4 oz	chopped dark chocolate	125 g
1 cup	heavy or whipping (35%) cream	250 mL

PEANUT BUTTER LAYER

1 cup	heavy or whipping (35%) cream	250 mL
2 tbsp	granulated sugar	30 mL
1 cup	smooth peanut butter	250 mL
4 tbsp	salted roasted peanuts	60 mL

1. *Chocolate Layer:* Place milk and dark chocolates in a large bowl. In a saucepan over medium heat, heat cream until it just starts to boil. Remove from heat and pour over chocolate. Using a spatula, slowly mix into chocolate until cream is completely incorporated and mixture is shiny. Pour into jars, dividing equally, and refrigerate for 2 hours.

2. *Peanut Butter Layer:* In a bowl, using electric mixer at high speed, beat cream and sugar to stiff peaks.

3. In another bowl, using electric mixer at medium speed, beat peanut butter for 2 minutes. Gently fold in whipped cream.

4. Transfer peanut butter mixture to pastry bag. Pipe over cooled chocolate preparation, dividing equally. Top with peanuts. Cover and refrigerate for at least 20 minutes or up to 4 hours.

Chocolate Hazelnut Cream Pudding

Like many of her friends, my daughter grew up demanding that Nutella be part of her daily diet. Any recipe made with this creamy, chocolaty product reminds members of that generation of their early years in a flash. When they get together, this is what my daughter makes.

Tip

Roasting hazelnuts brings out their distinct flavor and aroma. To roast hazelnuts, preheat oven to 350°F (180°C). Spread hazelnuts in a single layer on a baking sheet and place in preheated oven. Roast, stirring frequently, until lightly browned, about 8 minutes. Remove from oven and transfer to paper towels to cool. If the hazelnuts still have their skins, place them in a clean tea towel and rub them together; the skins will come off easily.

- Six 8-ounce (250 mL) jars
- Electric mixer

3 cups	heavy or whipping (35%) cream, divided	750 mL
⅔ cup	chocolate hazelnut spread	150 mL
5	egg yolks	5
½ cup	granulated sugar	125 mL
7 oz	dark (64%) chocolate, melted	210 mL
1 cup	chopped roasted hazelnuts (see Tips, left)	250 mL

1. In a saucepan, heat 2 cups (500 mL) cream just until it just begins to boil. Remove from heat and whisk in chocolate hazelnut spread, until combined. Cover and set aside for 5 minutes.

2. Meanwhile, in a large bowl, using electric mixer at medium speed, whisk egg yolks and sugar until thick and pale. Whisk in melted chocolate. Add reserved cream mixture and whisk until combined. Return to saucepan and cook over low heat for 8 minutes, stirring constantly, until smooth and thickened.

3. Remove from heat. Pour half the mixture into jars, dividing equally. Sprinkle with chopped hazelnuts, dividing equally. Refrigerate for 15 minutes. Set remaining pudding aside.

4. Meanwhile, in a bowl, using electric mixer with clean beaters at high speed, beat remaining cream until soft peaks form. Add to reserved pudding and whisk for 2 minutes. Carefully pour into jars. Refrigerate for at least 3 hours or up to 24 hours before serving.

Apricot, Chocolate Chip and Yogurt Treat

In my family we often argue that apricots are the best fruit on earth. Fresh apricots are an incredible combination of sweetness with a tart balance. There are several varieties of this sunny fruit. The plump reddish apricots from the Luberon region of France and those from Turkey are particularly delicious. Dried apricots have a different taste from fresh, but the two go very well together.

Tip

When purchasing dried apricots, try to get organically grown ones that have not been treated with sulfites. They might be a little brownish and look less appetizing, but they are free of pesticides and other chemicals.

- Four 8-ounce (250 mL) jars

½ cup	orange juice	125 mL
2 tsp	unflavored gelatin powder	10 mL
2 cups	vanilla yogurt	500 mL
2 tbsp	honey	30 mL
1 tsp	finely grated orange zest	5 mL
¼ cup	chopped dried apricots	60 mL
¼ cup	chocolate chips	60 mL
6	large fresh apricots, halved and pitted	6
	Mint leaves	

1. Place orange juice in a saucepan. Sprinkle with gelatin and set aside for 5 minutes. Transfer to stovetop and cook over low heat for 3 minutes, stirring, to dissolve gelatin. Remove from heat, pour into a bowl and set aside for 5 minutes.

2. Add yogurt, honey and orange zest and mix until well incorporated. Fold in dried apricots and chocolate chips. Refrigerate for 15 minutes.

3. Place one apricot half in each jar. Cover with half of the yogurt mixture, dividing equally. Add a second apricot half to each jar and cover with remaining yogurt mixture, dividing equally. Top with a final apricot half and refrigerate for at least 2 hours or up to 2 days.

4. Garnish each jar with a few mint leaves and serve.

Baked Chocolate Mousse

In winter I often make a batch of this dessert and keep it in my refrigerator in case unexpected guests show up for dinner (once cooked, it will keep for a week). If guests don't arrive, I have a great treat to enjoy whenever I feel the desire.

Tips

Always use fresh vanilla beans, which are soft and leathery and have a full aroma. Avoid brittle or dry vanilla beans, which are not fresh and will be difficult to cut open.

To avoid splashing boiling water, place the pan filled with jars on the oven rack, then fill with the water. Slide rack into oven.

- Preheat oven to 300°F (150°C)
- Four 8-ounce (250 mL) jars
- Electric mixer
- Baking pan large enough to accommodate the jars

⅔ cup	heavy or whipping (35%) cream	150 mL
1	vanilla bean, split lengthwise, seeds scraped out, pods and seeds reserved	1
⅓ cup	whole milk	75 mL
7 oz	chopped (70%) dark chocolate	210 g
2	egg yolks	2
¼ cup	granulated sugar	60 mL
2 tbsp	unsweetened cocoa powder	30 mL

1. In a saucepan over low heat, heat cream and reserved vanilla pod and seeds for 5 minutes. Set aside for 10 minutes to infuse flavor.

2. In a small saucepan, combine milk and chopped chocolate. Heat over low heat, whisking constantly, until chocolate is completely melted. Set aside.

3. In a bowl, using electric mixer at medium speed, beat egg yolks and sugar until mixture is pale and thick. Add vanilla cream mixture, beating constantly. Add melted chocolate mixture and beat until well combined.

4. Pour into jars, dividing equally. Cover tops with foil. Place jars in baking pan and add enough water to come halfway up the sides of the jars. Bake in preheated oven for 45 minutes. Remove jars from water and place on a rack to cool completely. Cover with plastic wrap and refrigerate for at least 8 hours or up to a week.

5. When you're ready to serve, sprinkle with cocoa powder and serve immediately.

Variations

Baked Chocolate Mousse with Rum: Add 3 tbsp (45 mL) dark rum along with the egg yolks and sugar in Step 3.

Baked Chocolate Mousse with Mint: I sometimes add ¼ cup (60 mL) crème de menthe liqueur to the egg yolk mixture in Step 3. It gives a nice crisp, cool taste to the chocolate.

Chocolate Hazelnut Cream Pudding (page 126)

Chocolate Tapioca (page 129)

Cantaloupe and Raspberry Splash (page 148)

Port Wine Jelly with Cookie Crunch (page 152)

Panna Cotta with Fresh Fruits and Chocolate Sauce (page 160)

Chocolate and Orange Liqueur Iced Soufflé (page 184)

Cold Strawberry Orange Soup (page 195)

Peach and Mango Parfait (page 198)

Pink Chantilly with Cranberries (page 201)

Raspberry and Coconut Fool (page 202)

Cherry Berry Smoothie (page 203)

Iced Mocha Syllabub (page 208)

Chocolate Tapioca

Makes 4 servings

For many years tapioca pudding seemed to have fallen out of favor, but in recent years it has been making a comeback. I'm seeing it more frequently on restaurant menus, which is a positive development. In addition to being delicious, this recipe is very quick to prepare.

Tips

To extract the seeds from a vanilla bean, use a small knife to split the pod lengthwise and scrape out the seeds.

Dark chocolate is preferred in this recipe for its sharp taste and low sugar content. Semisweet chocolate chips can be used instead, although they are much sweeter. You can also use organic 75% chocolate drops or chips.

Make Ahead

This dessert may be refrigerated, covered, for up to 24 hours. When you're ready to serve, complete Step 3.

• Four 8-ounce (250 mL) jars

2 cups	whole milk	500 mL
1/4 cup	granulated sugar	60 mL
3 tbsp	quick-cooking tapioca	45 mL
1	vanilla bean, split lengthwise, seeds scraped out, pod and seeds reserved (see Tips, left)	1
1	large egg	1
Pinch	salt	Pinch
1 cup	prepared chocolate syrup, divided	250 mL
1/2 cup	dark chocolate chips (see Tips, left)	125 mL

1. In a saucepan, combine milk, sugar, tapioca, vanilla pod and seeds, egg and salt. Cook over low heat, stirring, until mixture comes to a boil. Remove from heat. Remove vanilla pod and discard. Fold in 1/2 cup (125 mL) chocolate syrup. Set aside for 20 minutes, stirring often.

2. Fold in chocolate chips. Transfer to jars, dividing equally. Cover with plastic wrap, pressing down on the surface of the puddings to prevent a skin from forming, and refrigerate for at least 30 minutes or up to 24 hours.

3. When you're ready to serve, pour remaining chocolate syrup over the top.

Grandma's Tapioca

When I was kid, I wouldn't eat my grandmother's tapioca pudding. In fact, I never cared for it until I was old enough to enjoy it with a dash of dark rum. But now I've come to appreciate this old favorite for what it is — pure comfort food.

Tips

Shred the apples just before using them, so they do not brown. Or use Cortland apples, which do not brown.

Spiced rum is available in most liquor stores. To make spiced rum at home, add 2 cloves, 1 vanilla bean, 1 cinnamon stick and 1 tbsp (15 mL) freshly grated nutmeg to 4 cups (1 L) dark rum. Set aside to steep for 3 days. Strain, discarding solids, and it is ready to use.

- Four 8-ounce (250 mL) jars

1	large egg, beaten	1
1 cup	sweetened condensed milk	250 mL
2 cups	milk	500 mL
½ cup	granulated sugar	125 mL
¼ cup	quick-cooking tapioca	60 mL
1 tsp	vanilla extract	5 mL
½ cup	shredded apples	125 mL
Pinch	cinnamon	Pinch
½ cup	spiced dark rum, optional (see Tips, left)	125 mL

1. In a saucepan, combine egg, condensed milk, milk, sugar and tapioca. Set aside for 10 minutes.

2. Transfer saucepan to stovetop over medium heat and bring to a boil, stirring constantly. Add vanilla, apples and cinnamon. Cover and turn off heat. Let sit for 5 minutes.

3. Transfer to a bowl and mix well. Cover and let cool completely. Pour into jars, dividing equally. Cover with plastic wrap, placing it directly on surface of puddings. Refrigerate for 3 hours or up to 2 days.

4. When you are ready to serve, add 2 tbsp (30 mL) spiced rum, if using, to each jar.

Cold Ricotta and Raisin Pudding

This is a very easy dessert to prepare. Adding ice cream makes it particularly creamy.

Tip

To soften the ice cream, place it in the refrigerator for 30 minutes.

- Six 10-ounce (300 mL) jars

2 cups	ricotta cheese	500 mL
¼ cup	granulated sugar	60 mL
1 tsp	vanilla extract	5 mL
1 tbsp	finely grated lemon zest	15 mL
½ cup	golden raisins	125 mL
½ cup	dark currants (Corinth raisins)	125 mL
4	slices raisin bread, crusts removed, toasted and cut into long strips	4
2 cups	softened vanilla ice cream (see Tip, left)	500 mL

1. In a large bowl, using an electric mixer, beat ricotta and sugar for 2 minutes. Add vanilla extract and lemon zest. Fold in currants and raisins. Refrigerate for 10 minutes.

2. Add softened ice cream to ricotta preparation and, using a spatula, mix delicately. Pour into jars, dividing equally.

3. Serve with strips of raisin toast.

Variations

Replace the raisins with an equal quantity of dried cherries or cranberries.

Coconut Cream Dream

I love coconut. I put it in my bath, in my hair, in my soups and, of course, in my desserts. I have a friend who is allergic to eggs, and since traditional coconut pies contain eggs, she can't enjoy them. I developed this recipe for her and she loves it!

Tips

Make sure to use coconut cream, which comes in a can labelled as such. It is thick and creamy. If you only have coconut milk, drain off the clear liquid from the top of the can and use the creamy part at the bottom.

Always store coconut in the refrigerator to keep it fresh.

Make Ahead

Toasting the coconut can be done up to 2 days in advance. Store toasted coconut in an airtight container at room temperature.

- Preheat oven to 350°F (180°C)
- Six 8-ounce (250 mL) jars
- Electric mixer

¼ cup	shredded coconut	60 mL
2 cups	coconut cream, chilled overnight in the refrigerator	500 mL
1 tsp	vanilla extract	5 mL
1 tsp	finely grated lime zest	5 mL
4	eggs	4
¼ cup	confectioner's (icing) sugar	60 mL
½ cup	heavy or whipping (35%) cream	125 mL
½ cup	granulated sugar	125 mL
Pinch	ground nutmeg	Pinch

1. Place shredded coconut on a baking sheet and bake in preheated oven for 7 minutes. Remove from oven, stir well and return to oven for 7 minutes. Remove from oven and set aside to cool completely.

2. In a chilled bowl, using electric mixer at medium speed, beat coconut cream until fluffy. Add vanilla and lime zest, then gradually beat in confectioner's sugar. Fold in half the reserved toasted coconut.

3. Transfer to jars, dividing equally. Tap the jars on the counter to eliminate air bubbles. Refrigerate for at least 15 minutes or up to 2 hours.

4. In a bowl, using electric mixer with clean beaters at high speed, whip cream, granulated sugar and nutmeg to stiff peaks. Fold in remaining toasted coconut. Spoon mixture overtop chilled custards. Refrigerate for 30 minutes and serve.

Peach-Spiked Rice Pudding

An old French recipe for rice pudding called *abricots à la Condé* pairs rice with apricots and vanilla. Condé was a prince who lived in the Château de Chantilly, and his extravagant gastronomic feasts inspired his chef, the famous Vatel, to invent many recipes that still bear his name, as well as that of the château — for instance, crème chantilly. My recipe is made with canned peaches in syrup, making it easy to prepare all year round. I like to add a bit of rum and orange blossom water to spice up the pleasure.

Tip

Use canned peach halves in syrup. Drain the peaches, reserving the syrup for the sauce.

Make Ahead

The rice pudding can be prepared up to one day ahead of when you intend to serve it.

The sauce can be prepared the day before and reheated on low heat before serving.

- Six 8-ounce (250 mL) wide-mouth jars

RICE PUDDING

½ cup	short-grain rice, rinsed in warm water and drained	125 mL
3 cups	half-and-half (10%) cream	750 mL
¼ cup	granulated sugar	60 mL
1	vanilla bean, split lengthwise, seeds scraped out, pod and seeds reserved	1
1 tsp	salt	5 mL
2	egg yolks	2
2 tbsp	sour cream	30 mL
1 tbsp	unsalted butter	15 mL
1 tsp	orange blossom water, optional	5 mL
6	canned peach halves (see Tips, left)	6

SAUCE

2 cups	apricot preserves	500 mL
¼ cup	peach syrup (from drained peaches)	60 mL
¼ cup	water	60 mL
2 tbsp	dark rum	30 mL

1. *Rice Pudding:* In a saucepan, combine rice, half-and-half, sugar, vanilla pod and seeds and salt. Bring to a boil over medium heat, stirring constantly. Lower heat and simmer, stirring often, for 30 minutes or until liquid is absorbed and mixture is thick.

2. Remove from heat. Remove vanilla pod and discard. Add egg yolks, sour cream, butter and orange blossom water, if using; mix vigorously to incorporate quickly.

3. Pour into jars, filling halfway. Place 1 peach half in each jar and lightly press it into the pudding. Cover jars and refrigerate for at least 3 hours or up to 1 day.

4. *Sauce:* In a saucepan, combine apricot preserves, peach syrup, water and rum. Cook over medium heat, stirring, for about 7 minutes or until just beginning to boil. Remove from heat and set aside to cool for 5 minutes. Pour over rice pudding and serve immediately.

Variation

For a more traditional recipe, replace the peaches with canned apricots in syrup. You will need 12 halves.

Cranberries and Orange Custard

Makes 8 servings

Rich in color, cranberries are an unbeatable winter treat. The orange flavor emphasizes their tartness, and both flavors highlight the mellow custard.

Tip

A package of flavored gelatin powder contains about 3 oz (90 g) of powder. For this recipe, use about half. Keep the remainder to make jelly.

- Eight 8-ounce (250 mL) jars

ORANGE CUSTARD

2 cups	freshly squeezed orange juice, divided	500 mL
3 tbsp	orange-flavored gelatin powder (see Tip, left)	45 mL
½ cup	plain low-fat Greek yogurt	125 mL
¾ cup	heavy or whipping (35%) cream	175 mL
½ cup	liquid honey, divided	125 mL
Pinch	salt	Pinch

CRANBERRIES

2 cups	fresh or frozen cranberries, divided	500 mL
2 tbsp	finely grated orange zest	30 mL
½ cup	water	125 mL

1. *Orange Custard:* Pour ⅓ cup (75 mL) orange juice into a small bowl and sprinkle with gelatin. Set aside for 5 minutes.

2. In a large bowl, whisk yogurt into remaining orange juice.

3. In a saucepan over medium heat, combine cream, 2 tbsp (30 mL) honey and salt; bring to a simmer. Whisk in gelatin mixture and cook, stirring, until gelatin dissolves completely. Pour into yogurt mixture and whisk for 2 minutes, until very smooth. Pour into jars, dividing equally.

4. *Cranberries:* Top each jar with a few cranberries (they will fall to the bottom of the custard) and refrigerate for 4 hours or overnight.

5. In a saucepan, combine remaining honey, remaining cranberries, orange zest and water. Cook over medium heat for 20 minutes, until cranberries pop and liquid has reduced by half. Remove from heat and set aside to cool for 15 minutes. Pour over custards and serve immediately.

Orange and Kiwi Yogurt Pudding

Today, thanks to the availability of exotic fruits all year long, oranges and kiwis are part of our daily diet. But not so long ago, I can remember eating my first kiwi. Saffron is not often used in desserts, but it adds an interesting touch to fruit.

Tips

Although orange-blossom honey will intensify the orange flavor in the pudding, any good liquid honey will work well.

Navel oranges are excellent eating oranges that peel easily. They are a bit less juicy than other varieties but have seedless segments that are easily removed from the membrane and hold their shape well.

Kiwifruit cannot be added to gelatin, since it belongs to the family of fruits that prevent gelatin from setting. Pineapple, guava and mango and kiwi all need to be cooked before being added to gelatin.

- Six 8-ounce (250 mL) jars
- Food processor

YOGURT PUDDING

3 cups	plain full-fat yogurt	750 mL
1/2 cup	granulated sugar	125 mL
1/4 tsp	vanilla extract	1 mL
Pinch	ground cardamom	Pinch
1/8 tsp	saffron	0.5 mL
1 cup	freshly squeezed orange juice,	250 mL
2 tbsp	unflavored gelatin powder	30 mL
1 tbsp	finely grated orange zest	15 mL

ORANGE AND KIWI SYRUP

6	kiwifruit, peeled and sliced, divided	6
1/4 cup	freshly squeezed orange juice	60 mL
1 tbsp	liquid honey, preferably orange-blossom	15 mL
1	navel orange, segmented (see Tips, left and page 21)	1

1. *Yogurt Pudding:* In a bowl, whisk together yogurt, sugar, vanilla, cardamom and saffron, until sugar is dissolved.

2. Pour orange juice into a saucepan and sprinkle gelatin over the top. Set aside for 5 minutes to soften, then heat over low heat, stirring, until gelatin dissolves. Whisk into yogurt mixture and fold in orange zest. Pour into jars, dividing equally. Cover and refrigerate for at least 2 hours or up to 48 hours.

3. *Orange and Kiwi Syrup:* In food processor fitted with the metal blade, purée 5 of the kiwis. Set aside.

4. In a saucepan over medium heat, bring orange juice and honey to a simmer. Cook, stirring constantly, for 3 minutes. Add orange segments and reserved kiwi purée and cook, stirring carefully, for 2 minutes. Remove from heat and set aside to cool for 15 minutes.

5. Spoon orange and kiwi syrup over puddings, dividing equally. Top with kiwi slices and serve immediately.

Lemon Custard with Grapefruit Syrup

Makes 6 servings

This is a delicate, lemony custard — one that does not cause your mouth to pucker. Adding fragrant verbena leaves balances the citrus beautifully.

Tips

If lemon verbena is not available, substitute an equal quantity of lemon balm leaves.

To avoid splashing boiling water, place the pan filled with jars on the oven rack, then fill with the water. Slide rack into oven.

- Preheat oven to 325°F (160°C)
- Six 8-ounce (250 mL) jars
- Electric mixer
- Baking pan large enough to accommodate the jars

CUSTARD

1 cup	heavy or whipping (35%) cream	250 mL
1 cup	whole milk	250 mL
1 cup	chopped lemon verbena leaves	250 mL
¾ cup	granulated sugar, divided	175 mL
2	large eggs	2
3	large egg yolks	3
¼ cup	finely grated lemon zest	60 mL

GRAPEFRUIT SYRUP

2 cups	grapefruit juice	500 mL
2 tbsp	finely grated grapefruit zest	30 mL
2 cups	granulated sugar	500 mL

1. *Custard:* In a saucepan, combine cream, milk, lemon verbena and half of the sugar. Bring to a simmer over low heat (do not boil), whisking and crushing the leaves with the whisk. Cook for 5 minutes. Place a strainer over a bowl and strain, discarding solids. Set liquid aside.

2. In a large bowl, using electric mixer at medium speed, whisk eggs, egg yolks and remaining sugar until pale and thick. Slowly add ½ cup (125 mL) of the cream mixture, beating constantly. Add to remaining cream mixture in saucepan. Add lemon zest and mix well.

3. Pour mixture into jars, dividing equally. Place jars in baking pan, evenly spaced apart and not touching the sides of the pan, and add enough boiling water to come halfway up the sides of the jars. Cover pan with aluminum foil, piercing a few holes in the top.

Make Ahead

The individual components can be prepared up to 2 days ahead and refrigerated separately. Combine the lemon custard and the syrup when you're ready to serve.

4. Bake in preheated oven for 15 minutes. Remove foil and continue baking for 20 minutes or until custards are just set. Remove from oven. Transfer jars to a wire rack and set aside until cool. Cover and refrigerate for at least 6 hours or up to 2 days.

5. *Grapefruit Syrup:* In a saucepan, combine grapefruit juice and zest and sugar. Bring to a boil over medium heat, stirring constantly. Reduce heat and simmer for 10 minutes, until syrupy. Transfer to a glass container, cover and refrigerate for at least 4 hours or up to 2 days.

6. When you're ready to serve, pour grapefruit syrup over custards, dividing evenly. Serve immediately.

Limoncello and Blood Orange Cream

Limoncello is a liqueur made from lemon rind. The best version is made with the famous Amalfi lemons. It is served chilled after meals. I was lucky enough to discover limoncello on a very warm night in Rome, after I'd just eaten the best pizza of my life.

Tips

If you do not have a fresh blood orange on hand, replace the blood orange zest with an equal quantity of zest from a navel orange.

Bottled blood orange juice is available all year long in fine food shops. When blood oranges are in season, squeeze your own.

Keep your bottle of limoncello in the freezer (like vodka) and serve it in small glasses after a meal, or over vanilla ice cream.

Use the quantity of limoncello that suits your taste: a smaller amount if you are not a fan and a larger one if you are looking for strong flavor.

- Six 8-ounce (250 mL) jars
- Electric mixer

2 cups	heavy or whipping (35%) cream, divided	500 mL
½ cup	whole milk	125 mL
3 tbsp	finely grated blood orange zest	45 mL
2 cups	blood orange juice (see Tips, left)	500 mL
1 tbsp	packed brown sugar	15 mL
5	large egg yolks	5
1 cup	granulated sugar	250 mL
¾ to 1½ cups	cold limoncello, divided	175 to 375 mL

1. In a saucepan, combine 1 cup (250 mL) cream, milk and orange zest. Bring to a boil, cover and remove from heat. Set aside to steep for 40 minutes.

2. In a small saucepan over medium heat, bring orange juice and brown sugar to a boil. Reduce heat and simmer for 30 minutes. Remove from heat and set aside to cool completely. Stir in 3 tbsp (45 mL) limoncello.

3. In a bowl, using electric mixer at medium speed, beat egg yolks and granulated sugar until thick and pale.

4. Return cream mixture to stovetop and heat for 2 minutes without boiling. Slowly add half of the warm mixture to egg yolk mixture and beat for 2 minutes. Add egg yolk mixture to the saucepan with the remaining cream. Cook over low heat, stirring constantly, until thick enough to coat the back of a spoon. Remove from heat. Stir in reserved blood orange syrup.

5. Pour remaining limoncello into jars, dividing equally. Add orange cream, dividing equally. Refrigerate for at least 4 hours or up to 24 hours.

Pomegranate and Cream Cheese Dipper

Makes 4 servings

This creamy treat makes a lovely dessert accompanied by fruit or cookies to dip.

Tip

Pomegranate seeds can be bought fresh or frozen in supermarkets or specialty food shops.

Make Ahead

This dip can be prepared and refrigerated for up to 2 days before serving. Complete Step 1. Allow to come to room temperature and then whip for 30 seconds before serving. Transfer to jars.

- Four 8-ounce (250 mL) jars
- Food processor

2 cups	softened cream cheese, at room temperature	500 g
6 tbsp	unsalted butter, at room temperature	90 mL
1 cup	sour cream	250 mL
1/2 cup	confectioner's (icing) sugar, sifted	125 mL
1 cup	pomegranate juice	250 mL
1/4 cup	pomegranate seeds	60 mL
	Cookies	
	Sliced fruit	

1. In food processor fitted with the metal blade, process cream cheese and butter until fluffy. Add sour cream and sugar and pulse several times to blend. Add pomegranate juice and process for 1 minute. Add pomegranate seeds and pulse once or twice, just enough to integrate.

2. Spoon mixture into jars, dividing equally, and refrigerate for 30 minutes. Serve with cookies and fruit slices for dipping.

Soft Almond Nougat

Makes 8 servings

In my life as a confiseur I loved making all kinds of nougat. Nougat has to be one of the oldest sweet treats. Made with a base of egg whites, almonds and honey, it goes back to the 15th century in Italy. Here is a quick and easy way to enjoy the pleasure of mild-tasting nougat in a jar. Use small jars, for it is very sweet and satisfies quickly.

Tips

When incorporating warm ingredients into beaten egg whites, it is better to proceed slowly and raise the speed as the mixture blends. This incorporates air slowly and helps to cool the warm ingredients (in this case honey), producing a much more stable texture.

When beating egg whites into meringue, use fresh eggs and leave them out at room temperature for 1 hour before beating to maximize volume.

Make Ahead

This dessert can be made up to 2 hours ahead of when you plan to serve it. Cover and chill.

- Eight 6-ounce (175 mL) jars (see Tips, left)
- Microwave oven
- Electric mixer

8 tsp	apricot jam	40 mL
2	large egg whites	2
1 cup	liquid honey	250 mL
1 cup	heavy or whipping (35%) cream	250 mL
½ tsp	almond extract	2 mL
¾ cup	chopped toasted almonds	175 mL
1 tbsp	finely grated orange zest	15 mL

1. Spoon 1 tsp (5 mL) apricot jam into each jar.

2. Place honey in a microwave-safe bowl and heat on High for 1 minute. Stir well and heat for an additional minute.

3. In a large bowl, using electric mixer at high speed, beat egg whites to soft peaks. Reduce speed to low and add warm honey, whisking slowly at first and increasing the speed every 2 minutes, until stiff peaks form, about 6 minutes.

4. In another bowl, using clean beaters, beat cream and almond extract until soft peaks form. Fold into egg white mixture along with almonds and orange zest. Spoon into jars. Cover and refrigerate for at least 30 minutes or up to 2 hours before serving.

Variation

Soft Hazelnut Nougat: Substitute the almonds with an equal quantity of toasted hazelnuts.

Fig and Lavender Cream

Lavender is often associated with perfume but this fragrant plant is also exquisite in food. It brings an original twist to all fruits and creamy desserts.

Tip

Be careful to buy real edible lavender from a fine grocery shop or organic supplier. Sometimes people mistake other purple garden plants (such as lavendin) that are not edible for lavender.

• Eight 8-ounce (250 mL) jars

3 cups	heavy or whipping (35%) cream	750 mL
1 cup	mascarpone cheese	250 mL
1 cup	lavender honey, divided	250 mL
3	large egg yolks	3
Pinch	salt	Pinch
18	fresh ripe black figs, quartered	18
4	sprigs lavender, divided (see Tips, left)	4

1. In a cold bowl, whisk together cream and mascarpone to form soft peaks. Add $1/2$ cup (125 mL) honey and continue to whisk until stiff peaks form. Refrigerate for 1 hour.

2. In a large, heatproof bowl placed over a pan of simmering water, whisk remaining honey, egg yolks and salt until pale and thick. Remove from heat. Whisk in half the mascarpone mixture. Add figs and gently mix. Pour into jars, dividing equally (jars should be about half full).

3. Add the flowers of 2 of the lavender sprigs to the remaining mascarpone mixture. Spoon into jars. Refrigerate for 30 minutes. Garnish with remaining lavender sprigs and serve.

Not Your Mother's Jell-O

Pistachio and Sour Cream Jelly

The first time I tasted pistachios was in Sicily, where they develop their sunny taste in a perfect climate and lend it to the best ice cream ever. In this recipe, the sour cream jelly brings out their full flavor.

Tips

It is worth getting the best ice cream for this dessert — it will make a difference.

A double boiler is a hot-water bath that creates a gentle heat around food. It is the best way to heat a preparation very gently without burning it. To make a double boiler, place a heat-resistant bowl over a saucepan half-filled with simmering (not boiling) water. The bowl should fit inside the saucepan, sitting neatly on its rim, with its base never touching the water.

- Six 8-ounce (250 mL) jars
- Electric mixer

JELLY

3 tbsp	unflavored gelatin powder	45 mL
1/4 cup	cold water	60 mL
2 cups	sour cream	500 mL
1 cup	pistachio ice cream	250 mL
1 cup	granulated sugar	250 mL
1 tbsp	rum	15 mL
1 tsp	vanilla extract	5 mL
1 cup	heavy or whipping (35%) cream	250 mL
1 cup	pistachio ice cream	250 mL
1/4 cup	chopped shelled pistachios	60 mL

1. In a small, heatproof bowl, sprinkle gelatin over cold water. Set aside for 5 minutes. Place bowl over simmering water (see Tips, left) and whisk until gelatin is completely dissolved. Set aside for 10 minutes.

2. In a bowl, using electric mixer at medium speed, beat sour cream, pistachio ice cream, sugar, rum and vanilla until thick and fluffy. Add gelatin mixture and beat for 2 minutes. Set aside.

3. In another bowl, using electric mixer with clean beaters at high speed, beat cream until stiff peaks form. Gently fold into sour cream mixture. Spoon into jars, dividing equally. Refrigerate for at least 6 hours or up to 2 days.

4. Top each jar with a scoop of pistachio ice cream. Garnish with chopped pistachios and serve immediately.

Vegetarian Gelatin

Gelatin powder is made from animal products. If you are a vegetarian, you will want to substitute an appropriate alternative. In my opinion the most suitable replacement is agar-agar, a colorless sea vegetable (seaweed) also known as kanten. It is available in natural foods stores and Asian markets. Unlike gelatin, agar-agar does not bloom in water. It needs to be stirred into hot liquid and come to a full boil for 3 to 5 minutes. If substituting agar-agar for gelatin in any recipe in this book, follow the manufacturer's instructions. Many brands of kosher gelatin (flavored or unflavored) are suitable for vegans — check the label and follow the manufacturer's instructions.

Cherry Jubilee with Wine Jelly

As a summer treat, nothing beats cherries jubilee. As a child I thought of it as a grown-up dessert, and as a result my interest was piqued. I was allowed to eat only the ice cream from my mother's bowl, but the flavorful kirsch syrup was the best part. This dessert is very easy to make, but what a finale to any meal!

Tips

You will need about 2½ cups (625 mL) of pitted cherries for this recipe.

When flambéing the cherries, wear oven mitts to protect your hands from the flame.

Make Ahead

The wine jelly can be made up to 3 days before you intend to serve this dessert.

- Four 10-ounce (300 mL) jars
- Fine-mesh sieve

WINE JELLY

¾ cup	cold water	175 mL
¼ cup	unflavored gelatin powder	60 mL
½ cup	granulated sugar	125 mL
2½ cups	dry red wine	625 mL

CHERRY TOPPING

3 tbsp	unsalted butter	45 mL
3 cups	large cherries, pitted (see Tips, left)	750 mL
½ cup	granulated sugar	125 mL
¼ cup	Kirsch	60 mL
2 cups	vanilla ice cream	500 mL

1. *Wine Jelly:* Place water in a large bowl and sprinkle with gelatin. Set aside for 5 minutes.

2. Meanwhile, in a saucepan, combine sugar and wine. Bring to a boil over medium heat. Reduce heat and simmer until sugar is completely dissolved. Add gelatin mixture and whisk until dissolved. Cook for 1 minute. Remove from heat and pour through a fine-mesh sieve into a large bowl. Set aside to cool for 15 minutes. Pour into jars, dividing equally. Refrigerate for at least 4 hours, until set. Cover and refrigerate for up to 3 days.

3. *Cherry Topping:* In a large skillet over medium heat, melt butter. Add cherries and sugar; cook over medium heat, stirring, until sugar is dissolved. Continue to cook, stirring often, for 7 minutes or until cherries are just tender and their skins are crinkled. Remove from heat. Add Kirsch and, standing well back, ignite. Remove from heat and shake pan until flame is extinguished.

4. *Assembly:* Place a scoop of vanilla ice cream over wine jelly in each jar. Cover with warm cherries and serve.

Variations

White wine, dry or sweet, can be used instead of red wine. A mixture of half port wine and half red wine can also be used for a special treat.

Grape Jubilee with Wine Jelly: Substitute an equal quantity of seedless red grapes for the cherries.

Lychee Mousse and Orange Jelly

What a blessing to have lychee fruit available all year long. It makes delightful desserts. Pairing lychees with a delicate orange jelly adds a refreshing buzz.

Tips

You will need two 20-ounce (530 mL) cans of lychees to make this recipe.

If they're available, use fresh lychees.

Make Ahead

The orange jelly can be prepared up to 2 days before you intend to serve it.

- Six 8-ounce (250 mL) jars
- Food processor
- Electric mixer
- Rimmed baking sheet

ORANGE JELLY

2	packages (each 3 oz/85 g) orange-flavored gelatin powder	1
1 cup	hot water	250 mL
1 cup	cold orange juice	250 mL
½ tsp	ground ginger	2 mL

LYCHEE MOUSSE

2 tbsp	unflavored gelatin powder	30 mL
¼ cup	cold water	60 mL
3 cups	canned lychees in syrup, divided	750 mL
1 cup	heavy or whipping (35%) cream	250 mL
3 tbsp	confectioner's sugar, plus additional for dusting	45 mL

1. *Orange Jelly:* In a large bowl, dissolve orange-flavored gelatin in hot water. Whisk in orange juice and ginger. Pour into jars, dividing equally. Screw on lids or cover tightly with aluminium foil secured with an elastic or silicone band. Place jars on baking sheet, on their sides but slightly tilted, so the jelly can set on one side of the jar, and refrigerate for at least 4 hours, until set.

2. *Lychee Mousse:* In a saucepan, sprinkle unflavored gelatin over cold water and set aside to soften, about 5 minutes. Cook over medium heat, whisking, until gelatin is dissolved (do not boil). Remove from heat and set aside to cool completely.

3. Drain lychees and reserve syrup for another use. Set 6 lychees aside for garnish. Place drained lychees in food processor and purée. Transfer to a large bowl and stir in softened gelatin.

4. Using electric mixer at high speed, beat cream and confectioner's sugar to stiff peaks. Gently fold whipped cream into lychee mixture. Spoon into jars alongside the orange jelly, dividing equally. Refrigerate for 2 hours.

5. When you're ready to serve, garnish jars with reserved lychees and sprinkle with confectioner's sugar.

Watermelon and Lime Aspic

I remember long, warm summer days when, out and about with my family, we enjoyed slices of fresh watermelon. It was a delicious, thirst-quenching delight. I also have fond memories of my mother's aspics, and I am so happy that aspics are coming back into style.

Tip

Always purchase watermelon whole. It should not be bruised, cut or dented.

- Six 10-ounce (300 mL) jars
- Food processor

1	large red watermelon, halved and seeded	1
1	small yellow watermelon, halved and seeded	1
1/2 cup	freshly squeezed lime juice	125 mL
2	packages (each 3 oz/ 85 g) lime-flavored gelatin powder, divided	2
1/2 cup	cold water	125 mL
1/2 cup	boiling water	125 mL
2 tbsp	finely grated lime zest	30 mL
1 tbsp	chopped mint leaves	15 mL
1 tbsp	confectioner's (icing) sugar	15 mL

1. Cut half of the red watermelon flesh into small cubes and set aside.

2. In food processor, purée remaining red watermelon until liquefied. Transfer to a large bowl and refrigerate.

3. Add yellow watermelon flesh to food processor and purée until liquefied. Transfer to a saucepan. Stir in lime juice and bring to a boil. Remove from heat and mix in 1 package lime-flavored gelatin. Add cold water and set aside for 5 minutes.

4. Pour into individual jars. Add reserved red watermelon cubes. Refrigerate for 2 hours.

5. In a bowl, combine remaining package of gelatin powder and boiling water. Mix well. Stir in reserved red watermelon purée and lime zest. Fold in mint. Pour into jars and refrigerate for 6 hours, until set.

6. Sprinkle lightly with confectioner's sugar and serve immediately.

Cantaloupe and Raspberry Splash

Summer cantaloupes (also known as muskmelons) are bursting with flavor, and when we see them at the market, we always buy extra. We eat the first few just as they come, to enjoy their unique taste, and the "extras" get transformed into pleasurable soups, creams and jellies or are paired with fresh raspberries for an unforgettable treat.

Tip

Chill the port wine in the freezer for 2 hours before serving. It provides a very refreshing finish for the dessert.

Make Ahead

The cantaloupe custards can be prepared and refrigerated up to 2 days in advance. Complete Steps 1 through 4, cover and refrigerate.

- Six 12-ounce (375 mL) jars
- Food processor or blender
- Fine-mesh sieve

RASPBERRIES

3 cups	raspberries, divided	750 mL
2 tbsp	liquid honey	30 mL

CANTALOUPE

2	large cantaloupes, peeled, seeded and diced	2
1 tbsp	unflavored gelatin powder (2 packets)	15 mL
1/2 cup	low-fat plain yogurt	125 mL
3/4 cup	heavy or whipping (35%) cream	175 mL
1/4 cup	granulated sugar	60 mL
Pinch	salt	Pinch
1 cup	cold port wine (see Tip, left)	250 mL
1/2 cup	chopped toasted pine nuts	125 mL

1. *Raspberries:* In a large bowl, combine raspberries and honey.

2. In food processor, purée 2 cups (500 mL) of the raspberry mixture. Transfer to a fine-mesh sieve set over a bowl and, using a wooden spoon, press to extract as much purée as possible. Discard seeds. Cover and refrigerate purée for at least 2 hours. Refrigerate remaining raspberries as well.

3. *Cantaloupe:* In food processor, purée cantaloupes until smooth. Place sieve over a bowl and, using a wooden spoon, press solids through. Spoon 1/2 cup (125 mL) purée into a small bowl and sprinkle with gelatin; set aside for 5 minutes. Add yogurt to remaining purée and stir well.

4. In a saucepan over medium heat, bring cream, sugar and salt to a simmer. Whisk in gelatin mixture and cook for 2 minutes or until gelatin is completely dissolved. Add to yogurt mixture and stir well. Divide equally among jars. Refrigerate for at least 4 hours, until set. Cover with plastic and refrigerate up to 2 days.

Tip

Use larger or smaller jars to make this recipe. Just be sure to divide the contents equally between the jars. If you prefer, recycle used jam or condiment jars to make this recipe.

5. *Assembly:* When you're ready to serve, spoon raspberry purée over cantaloupe custards, dividing equally. Garnish with whole raspberries, dividing equally, and top each jar with a splash of cold port wine. Garnish with pine nuts and serve immediately.

Variations

Cantaloupe and Strawberry Splash: Substitute an equal quantity of hulled strawberries for the raspberries, but be aware that strawberries are not as pleasantly tart and crisp as raspberries when paired with cantaloupe.

Watermelon and Raspberry Splash: Substitute watermelon for the cantaloupe for a much more subtle taste. Substitute melon liqueur (such as Midori) for the port wine.

Vegetarian Gelatin

Gelatin powder is made from animal products. If you are a vegetarian, you will want to substitute an appropriate alternative. In my opinion the most suitable replacement is agar-agar, a colorless sea vegetable (seaweed) also known as kanten. It is available in natural foods stores and Asian markets. Unlike gelatin, agar-agar does not bloom in water. It needs to be stirred into hot liquid and come to a full boil for 3 to 5 minutes. If substituting agar-agar for gelatin in any recipe in this book, follow the manufacturer's instructions. Many brands of kosher gelatin (flavored or unflavored) are suitable for vegans — check the label and follow the manufacturer's instructions.

Cider Jelly and Walnut Cream

I love walnuts and they pair well with brown sugar. This combination of cool jelly with a creamy topping is always a winner.

Tips

Sparkling "hard" cider can be replaced by non-alcoholic sparkling cider. Use cider without added sugar if possible.

Freezing the jars for an hour helps to retain the bubbles in bubbly jellies.

Walnuts go rancid quickly, so make sure yours are fresh. Buy in bulk from a purveyor with fast turnover or open the bag at the supermarket before buying — if the nuts smell rancid, complain. Walnuts should have a fresh, woody smell. Store them in the refrigerator or freezer.

The walnut cream can be used to garnish all kinds of cakes, puddings or pies. It can also be mixed with ice cream.

Make Ahead

The jelly can be prepared up to 2 days in advance.

- Four 8-ounce (250 mL) jars
- Food processor

JELLY

1 cup	granulated sugar	250 mL
¼ cup	cold water	60 mL
2	apples, peeled and shredded	2
¼ cup	unflavored gelatin powder	60 mL
¼ cup	cold unsweetened apple juice	60 mL
2 cups	cold dry sparkling cider, divided	500 mL

WALNUT CREAM

1 cup	chopped walnuts	250 mL
1 tbsp	packed brown sugar	15 mL
1 cup	mascarpone cheese	250 mL
3 tbsp	unsweetened apple juice	45 mL

1. Place jars in the freezer for 30 minutes.

2. *Jelly:* In a saucepan, combine sugar and water. Cook over low heat, stirring, until sugar is dissolved. Raise heat and bring to a boil. Remove from heat and stir in apples. Set aside for 5 minutes.

3. In a bowl, sprinkle gelatin over apple juice. Set aside for 5 minutes. Add to saucepan with apples and whisk until dissolved.

4. Slowly pour 1 cup (250 mL) cider into gelatin mixture. Stir lightly. Using a funnel, carefully pour into jars, dividing equally. Add remaining cider, dividing equally, and mix carefully to retain bubbles. Freeze jars for 1 hour (see Tips, left), then transfer to refrigerator for at least 6 hours or up to 2 days.

5. *Walnut Cream:* In food processor, process walnuts and brown sugar until nuts are coarsely chopped. Transfer to a skillet and cook, stirring, over medium heat until sugar is caramelizing. Remove from heat and set aside to cool.

6. In a bowl, whisk together mascarpone and apple juice. Fold in walnut mixture. Spoon over cider jelly and serve immediately.

Variation

Cider Jelly and Hazelnut Cream: Substitute an equal quantity of roasted hazelnuts for the walnuts.

Matcha Green Tea and Sesame Mousse

Makes 4 servings

I have a friend, a marine biologist, who lived in Japan for many years. She loves good food and came back with lots of recipes to share. One was a delicate matcha tea mousse. It makes a stunning statement with its unusual color and is very elegant to serve.

Tip

For a fancier version of this dessert, try spooning stewed cranberries overtop.

Make Ahead

This mousse can be prepared and refrigerated up to 2 days ahead.

- Four 6-ounce (175 mL) jars

¼ cup	water	60 mL
1 tbsp	unflavored gelatin powder	15 mL
1 cup	whole milk	250 mL
2	egg yolks	2
½ cup	granulated sugar	125 mL
1 tbsp	matcha green tea powder	15 mL
3 tbsp	warm water	45 mL
2 tbsp	black sesame seeds	30 mL
1 cup	heavy or whipping (35%) cream	250 mL

1. Place water in a small bowl and sprinkle with gelatin. Set aside for 5 minutes.

2. In a saucepan, heat milk (do not boil). Add gelatin and stir until melted.

3. In a bowl, using an electric mixer at medium speed, whisk egg yolks and sugar until mixture is pale and thick. Slowly add milk mixture, beating until well combined.

4. In a bowl, dissolve matcha powder in warm water. Add to milk mixture and stir well. Place bowl in a larger bowl filled with ice and cold water. Sprinkle with sesame seeds and whisk until cold.

5. In a cold bowl, using electric mixer with clean beaters, whip cream until stiff peaks form. Gently fold into tea mixture. Pour mousse into jars. Refrigerate for at least 3 hours, until thoroughly chilled, or up to 2 days before serving.

Port Wine Jelly with Cookie Crunch

Makes 4 servings

Like memories of good wine, food memories transform, adapt and get better with time. I once had the chance to drink a very old port (I think a 1949), and it was like drinking velvet. Since then, port has been one of my favorite drinks. I like to pair it with cheese, fruits and certain cookies. By adding brown sugar and pepper to this jelly, I can almost trick myself into thinking I'm once again experiencing that grand old port.

Tips

For best results, use good-quality port.

Using a funnel ensure that your jars will be filled neatly.

• Four 6-ounce (175 mL) jars

1½ cups	port wine	375 mL
1 tbsp	brown sugar	15 mL
1 tbsp	finely grated orange zest	15 mL
1 cup	freshly squeezed orange juice	250 mL
2 tsp	freshly ground black pepper	10 mL
1	piece (about 2 in/5 cm) cinnamon stick	1
1	clove	1
2	packages (each 3 oz/85 g) orange-flavored gelatin powder	2
8	gingersnap cookies, crushed	8

1. In a saucepan, combine port, brown sugar, orange zest and juice, pepper, cinnamon and clove. Cook over low heat for 4 minutes, until just beginning to boil. Cover and set aside for 30 minutes.

2. Strain mixture into a bowl. Discard solids and return liquid to saucepan. Cook over medium heat for 3 minutes to reheat. Remove from heat and pour in gelatin powder. Mix until dissolved.

3. Using a funnel, pour into jars, dividing equally, and refrigerate for at least 6 hours or until set. Or cover jars with plastic wrap and refrigerate for up to 48 hours.

4. When you're ready to serve, top with crushed gingersnaps. Serve immediately.

Vegetarian Gelatin

Gelatin powder is made from animal products. If you are a vegetarian, you will want to substitute an appropriate alternative. In my opinion the most suitable replacement is agar-agar, a colorless sea vegetable (seaweed) also known as kanten. It is available in natural foods stores and Asian markets. Unlike gelatin, agar-agar does not bloom in water. It needs to be stirred into hot liquid and come to a full boil for 3 to 5 minutes. If substituting agar-agar for gelatin in any recipe in this book, follow the manufacturer's instructions. Many brands of kosher gelatin (flavored or unflavored) are suitable for vegans — check the label and follow the manufacturer's instructions.

Hot Mango and Cilantro Jelly

A little mango, a little chile and a refreshing touch of cilantro — this dessert has the rhythm of a rumba. And that is exactly how it feels in your mouth when you taste this absolutely divine, fresh and sexy dessert. It's sure to please everyone.

Tips

Sweet wines such as French Vouvray or Sauternes or Italian Passito di Pantelleria are perfect for this recipe.

The jelly can be made and allowed to set in the jars up to 2 days before serving.

The mango mixture can be prepared several hours before serving, but don't add the mint leaves until the last minute.

- Four 8-ounce (250 mL) jars
- Fine-mesh sieve
- Food processor

4 tsp	unflavored gelatin powder	20 mL
2 cups	water	500 mL
3 tbsp	freshly squeezed lime juice	45 mL
1 cup	freshly squeezed orange juice	250 mL
1 cup	sweet white wine	250 mL
1 cup	granulated sugar	250 mL
1/2 cup	finely chopped cilantro leaves	125 mL
2	ripe mangoes, peeled, pitted and diced, divided	2
1	jalapeño pepper, seeded and finely chopped	1
1/4 cup	freshly squeezed orange juice	60 mL
1 tbsp	liquid honey	15 mL
1 tbsp	chopped fresh mint	15 mL

1. Place gelatin powder in a heatproof bowl. Add water, lime and orange juices and white wine; let stand for 10 minutes. Place bowl over a saucepan filled with simmering water and stir until gelatin has melted. Add sugar and stir until dissolved. Strain through sieve into a large bowl.

2. Add cilantro to gelatin mixture and stir well. Ladle immediately into jars, dividing equally. Add a few pieces of mango to each jar. Refrigerate for at least 3 hours or until set, or up to 2 days.

3. Half an hour before you're ready to serve, in a large bowl, combine remaining mango, jalapeño, orange juice and honey. Mix gently. Add mint and toss gently. Cover and refrigerate for 30 minutes.

4. When you're ready to serve, spoon mango mixture over the cilantro jelly.

Variation

You can substitute 1 tbsp (15 mL) finely chopped mint for the cilantro and about 5 peaches for the mangoes.

Melon in Raspberry Jelly

This is an old dessert I picked up from a friend who got it from her mother. It's the type of recipe people keep in little black books, and it's still remarkably fresh and colorful.

Tips

Be sure to buy ripe melons for a better-tasting result.

Using a funnel ensures that the jars will be filled neatly.

- Six 8-ounce (250 mL) tall jars
- Food processor
- Fine-mesh sieve

1	honeydew melon	1
¾ cup	granulated sugar, divided	175 mL
1 tbsp	freshly squeezed lemon juice	15 mL
¼ cup	cold water	60 mL
2 tsp	unflavored gelatin powder	10 mL
2 cups	frozen raspberries	500 mL
1 tsp	chopped fresh tarragon leaves	5 mL

1. Place jars on a baking sheet and refrigerate for 30 minutes.

2. Cut melon in half and remove seeds. Using a spoon, scoop out flesh from one half and transfer to food processor. Add ¼ cup (60 mL) sugar and the lemon juice and purée. Transfer to a bowl, cover and refrigerate.

3. Using a melon baller, remove flesh from second melon half. Transfer balls to a bowl as completed.

4. Pour water into a small bowl. Sprinkle with gelatin and set aside for 5 minutes.

5. In a microwaveable bowl, combine raspberries and remaining ½ cup (125 mL) sugar. Microwave on High for 1 minute. Stir, then microwave on High for 2 minutes. (Berries should be soft and have released their juices; if not, repeat for 15 seconds at a time.) Press berries through sieve placed over a saucepan. Discard seeds.

6. Bring raspberry liquid to a simmer over low heat. Stir in gelatin mixture and whisk until dissolved. Remove from heat and set aside for 5 minutes to cool. Stir in tarragon.

Tip

Use larger or smaller jars to make this recipe. Just be sure to divide the contents equally between the jars. If you prefer, recycle used jam or condiment jars to make this recipe.

Make Ahead

The jelly can be prepared up to 2 days ahead.

7. Using a funnel, pour into cold jars, filling halfway and dividing equally. Add melon balls and mix carefully. Refrigerate for at least 4 hours, until set, or up to 2 days. When you're ready to serve, pour cold melon sauce over jelly, dividing equally. Serve immediately.

Variation

If you can't find a honeydew melon, substitute with an equal quantity of cantaloupe.

Vegetarian Gelatin

Gelatin powder is made from animal products. If you are a vegetarian, you will want to substitute an appropriate alternative. In my opinion the most suitable replacement is agar-agar, a colorless sea vegetable (seaweed) also known as kanten. It is available in natural foods stores and Asian markets. Unlike gelatin, agar-agar does not bloom in water. It needs to be stirred into hot liquid and come to a full boil for 3 to 5 minutes. If substituting agar-agar for gelatin in any recipe in this book, follow the manufacturer's instructions. Many brands of kosher gelatin (flavored or unflavored) are suitable for vegans — check the label and follow the manufacturer's instructions.

Rose Jelly and Lemon Cream

Rose is an unusual flavor for most, but it's extremely addictive once you've tasted it. In India rose water is often used to flavor yogurt drinks and rice pudding. In Malaysia it is used as a flavoring for milk drinks. This is a delicate and surprising way to end a meal.

Tip

Rose syrup is not the same as rose water; it is made of strong rose water and sugar. Look for rose syrup in fine food shops. It can be used to flavor water, cocktails and milkshakes or simply served over ice cream. Once opened, store it in the refrigerator. The brand I usually use is Épicerie de Provence, but the most easily available brands are Monin and Teisseire.

• Four 8-ounce (250 mL) jars, chilled for 30 minutes

1	package (3 oz/85 g) raspberry-flavored gelatin powder	1
1 cup	boiling water	250 mL
1 cup	rose syrup (see Tip, left)	250 mL
½ cup	cold water	125 mL
1 cup	prepared lemon curd	250 mL
1 cup	sour cream	250 mL
2 tbsp	confectioner's (icing) sugar	30 mL

1. In a bowl, mix gelatin with boiling water. Set aside for 5 minutes. Mix in rose syrup and cold water. Using a funnel, transfer to jars, dividing equally. Refrigerate for at least 6 hours or until set.

2. When you're ready to serve, in a bowl, whisk together lemon curd and sour cream. Slowly add confectioner's sugar, whisking constantly until combined. Spoon lemon cream onto jellies and serve immediately.

Vegetarian Gelatin

Gelatin powder is made from animal products. If you are a vegetarian, you will want to substitute an appropriate alternative. In my opinion the most suitable replacement is agar-agar, a colorless sea vegetable (seaweed) also known as kanten. It is available in natural foods stores and Asian markets. Unlike gelatin, agar-agar does not bloom in water. It needs to be stirred into hot liquid and come to a full boil for 3 to 5 minutes. If substituting agar-agar for gelatin in any recipe in this book, follow the manufacturer's instructions. Many brands of kosher gelatin (flavored or unflavored) are suitable for vegans — check the label and follow the manufacturer's instructions.

Vanilla Panna Cotta

This traditional Italian dessert has become extremely popular in the past few years. Although it often appears on restaurant menus, nothing beats a homemade panna cotta. Just ask my husband, who can eat four at a time!

Tips

Serve with simple berries for an elegant dessert.

If you don't have 6-ounce (175 mL) jars, use larger or smaller ones to suit what you have on hand. Just be sure to divide the mixture equally among the jars.

- Six 6-ounce (175 mL) jars

¼ cup	cold water	60 mL
1 tbsp	unflavored gelatin powder	15 mL
1	vanilla bean, scraped out, seeds reserved	1
3 cups	heavy or whipping (35%) cream	750 mL
1 cup	granulated sugar	250 mL
1 tsp	vanilla extract	5 mL
	Fresh berries, optional	

1. Pour water into a saucepan and sprinkle with gelatin. Set aside to soften, about 10 minutes. Transfer to stovetop and add reserved vanilla seeds. Bring to a boil over low heat, stirring to dissolve gelatin. Remove from heat and set aside.

2. In a separate clean saucepan, combine cream and sugar. Over low heat, stir until sugar dissolves. Remove from heat. Add vanilla extract and reserved gelatin mixture. Pour into jars, dividing equally. Refrigerate overnight or for up to 3 days (if you are keeping it longer than overnight, cover loosely with plastic). When you are ready to serve, garnish with fresh berries, if using.

Coffee and Raspberry Panna Cotta

Makes 6 servings

Is this an unusual combination? Perhaps, but coffee and raspberries are a perfect match — both are bold and tart. Pairing them with yogurt enhances their tangy flavors.

Tip

Do not substitute regular instant coffee for the espresso powder, because instant coffee does not have the same rich, aromatic flavor. Instant coffee will make the taste bitter.

• Six 8-ounce (250 mL) jars

2 cups	crushed raspberries	500 mL
3 tbsp	packed brown sugar	45 mL
¼ cup	instant espresso powder	60 mL
1 cup	boiling water	250 mL
2½ tsp	unflavored gelatin powder	12 mL
¾ cup	nonfat vanilla yogurt	175 mL
¾ cup	heavy or whipping (35%) cream	175 mL
⅓ cup	granulated sugar	75 mL
½ tsp	vanilla extract	2 mL
⅛ tsp	ground cardamom	0.5 mL

1. In a saucepan, combine raspberries and brown sugar. Bring to boil, stirring constantly. Remove from heat and spoon into jars. Set aside.

2. In a microwave-safe bowl, combine espresso powder and boiling water. Sprinkle with gelatin and set aside for 5 minutes. Microwave on High for 20 seconds.

3. Meanwhile, in another bowl, whisk together yogurt, cream, granulated sugar, vanilla and cardamom. Add gelatin mixture and stir well.

4. Spoon into jars. Refrigerate overnight or for up to 3 days. Serve cold.

Vegetarian Gelatin

Gelatin powder is made from animal products. If you are a vegetarian, you will want to substitute an appropriate alternative. In my opinion the most suitable replacement is agar-agar, a colorless sea vegetable (seaweed) also known as kanten. It is available in natural foods stores and Asian markets. Unlike gelatin, agar-agar does not bloom in water. It needs to be stirred into hot liquid and come to a full boil for 3 to 5 minutes. If substituting agar-agar for gelatin in any recipe in this book, follow the manufacturer's instructions. Many brands of kosher gelatin (flavored or unflavored) are suitable for vegans — check the label and follow the manufacturer's instructions.

Lemon Lavender Panna Cotta

Makes 6 servings

The first time I saw a lavender field in full bloom, I cried. It was so incredibly beautiful. A few days later, I had my first taste of lavender ice cream. The magic of lavender had worked its enchantment again. In this recipe the flavor of the lavender must remain delicate to leave space for the freshness of the lemon. Simple to prepare, this dessert offers a spectacular surprise in terms of taste.

Tip

Make sure to buy edible lavender, as there are different types. The one for culinary use is also used in perfumes, but some used in perfumes is not suitable for eating. Do not use flowers from florists, nurseries or garden centers; in many cases they have been treated with pesticides. Buy lavender from an organic farmers' market or an organic food shop.

Make Ahead

The panna cotta can be made 2 days ahead and topped with lemon curd just before serving.

- Six 8-ounce (250 mL) jars
- Food processor

1 tbsp	dried edible lavender flowers (see Tip, left)	15 mL
¾ cup	granulated sugar, divided	175 mL
1 cup	whole milk, divided	250 mL
1 tbsp	unflavored gelatin powder	15 mL
2½ cups	heavy or whipping (35%) cream	625 mL
2 tbsp	finely grated lemon zest	30 mL
¼ tsp	vanilla extract	1 mL
1 cup	prepared lemon curd (see Tips, page 166)	250 mL

1. In food processor fitted with the metal blade, pulse lavender and ¼ cup (125 mL) sugar until combined. Transfer to a saucepan. Stir in ½ cup (125 mL) milk. Sprinkle with gelatin. Set aside for 15 minutes.

2. Meanwhile, in a large saucepan, combine cream, lemon zest, vanilla and remaining sugar and milk. Bring to a simmer over medium heat, whisking until sugar is dissolved. Remove from heat, cover and set aside for 10 minutes.

3. Return cream mixture to stovetop. Add gelatin mixture and stir until gelatin dissolves. Cook over medium heat for 2 minutes, but do not boil.

4. Pour into jars, dividing equally. Refrigerate for at least 6 hours or up to 2 days.

5. When you're ready to serve, top each jar with a dollop of lemon curd, dividing equally.

Panna Cotta with Fresh Fruit and Chocolate Sauce

This is my husband's absolute favorite dessert. I could make it every day and he would be happy. The beauty of this dessert is that you can vary the fresh fruit with the seasons.

Tip

Always use soft flesh vanilla beans. The dried ones are old and difficult to open. Vanilla pods can be placed in a large bowl of granulated sugar. Cover and store and you will always have vanilla sugar on hand.

Make Ahead

The panna cotta can be prepared up to 2 days in advance.

The chocolate sauce can be prepared up to 4 days before and reheated in the microwave for 1 minute. Cool before serving.

- Eight 10-ounce (300 mL) jars
- Small sieve

PANNA COTTA

6 tbsp	cold water	90 mL
4 tsp	unflavored gelatin powder	20 mL
4 cups	heavy or whipping (35%) cream	1 L
½ cup	granulated sugar	125 g
1	vanilla bean, split lengthwise, seeds scraped out and reserved (see Tip, left)	1
1 tsp	vanilla extract	5 mL

FRUIT

½ cup	passion fruit syrup (see Tips, page 161)	125 mL
8	strawberries, hulled and halved	8
16	raspberries	16
1	kiwifruit, peeled and diced	1
2	peaches, peeled and diced	2
1	banana, peeled and sliced	1
2 tbsp	granulated sugar	30 mL

CHOCOLATE SAUCE (see Tips, page 161)

2 cups	evaporated milk	500 mL
1 cup	granulated sugar	250 mL
¾ cup	unsweetened cocoa powder	175 mL
7 oz	dark (64 to 70%) chocolate, chopped	210 g

1. *Panna Cotta:* Place jars on a baking sheet and refrigerate for 30 minutes.

2. Pour water into a large bowl and sprinkle with gelatin. Set aside for 5 minutes.

3. In a saucepan, combine cream, sugar and vanilla pod and seeds. Stir well and set aside to infuse for 20 minutes. Place over medium heat and cook, stirring, until sugar dissolves completely. Remove from heat and stir in vanilla extract. Remove vanilla pod and discard. Pour warm mixture over gelatin and whisk until gelatin is completely dissolved.

Tips

Fruit syrups are available at supermarkets. Teisseire, Torani and Monin are common brands. If you can't find it, replace the passion-fruit syrup with an equal quantity of orange juice.

If you prefer, use your favorite prepared chocolate sauce.

4. Place small sieve over a jar and strain mixture into jar, filling to halfway. Repeat until all jars have been filled to halfway. Refrigerate for at least 3 hours, until set, or cover and refrigerate for up to 2 days.

5. *Fruit:* Pour passion fruit syrup into a bowl and add strawberries, raspberries, kiwi, peaches and banana. Sprinkle with sugar and toss gently. Cover and set aside for 1 hour.

6. *Chocolate Sauce:* In a saucepan, combine evaporated milk, sugar and cocoa powder. Whisk until well combined. Bring to a boil over medium heat. Lower heat and mix in chopped chocolate. Simmer for 3 minutes. Remove from heat and set aside to cool completely.

7. Pour a layer of cooled chocolate sauce over panna cotta. Using a slotted spoon, divide fruit mixture equally among jars (save the syrup for another use). Serve immediately.

Vegetarian Gelatin

Gelatin powder is made from animal products. If you are a vegetarian, you will want to substitute an appropriate alternative. In my opinion the most suitable replacement is agar-agar, a colorless sea vegetable (seaweed) also known as kanten. It is available in natural foods stores and Asian markets. Unlike gelatin, agar-agar does not bloom in water. It needs to be stirred into hot liquid and come to a full boil for 3 to 5 minutes. If substituting agar-agar for gelatin in any recipe in this book, follow the manufacturer's instructions. Many brands of kosher gelatin (flavored or unflavored) are suitable for vegans — check the label and follow the manufacturer's instructions.

Pomegranate Panna Cotta with Apricot Sauce

This is a colorful version of panna cotta. The apricot sauce brings a real zing to this creamy dessert. It is quickly prepared and can be kept in the refrigerator while you make the rest of the meal. It's always good to have your dessert ready ahead of time when you're having a dinner party.

Tip

Pomegranate seeds can be found fresh or frozen in supermarkets. If you prefer, remove them from fresh pomegranates.

Make Ahead

The panna cotta can be prepared up to 2 days before and kept refrigerated.

The sauce can be kept at room temperature for up to 3 hours.

- Six 8-ounce (250 mL) tall jars
- Small sieve

PANNA COTTA

¼ cup	cool water	60 mL
4 tsp	unflavored gelatin powder	20 mL
4 cups	heavy or whipping (35%) cream	1 L
¾ cup	granulated sugar	175 mL
½ cup	pomegranate juice	125 mL

APRICOT SAUCE

2 cups	chopped dried apricots	500 mL
2 cups	prepared chamomile tea	500 mL
2 tbsp	packed brown sugar	30 mL
½ cup	pomegranate seeds (see Tip, left)	125 mL

1. *Panna Cotta:* Place jars on a baking sheet and refrigerate for 30 minutes.

2. Pour water into a large bowl and sprinkle with gelatin. Set aside for 5 minutes.

3. In a large saucepan, combine cream and sugar. Heat over medium heat, stirring, until sugar dissolves completely. Pour mixture over reserved gelatin and whisk until gelatin is completely dissolved. Stir in pomegranate juice.

4. Place sieve over one jar and strain mixture into jar, filling to halfway. Repeat until all jars have been filled halfway. Refrigerate for at least 4 hours, until set, or for up to 2 days.

5. *Apricot Sauce:* In a saucepan, combine apricots, chamomile tea and brown sugar. Heat over low heat, stirring, until sugar is dissolved. Continue to cook, stirring often, for 20 minutes, until thickened. Fold in pomegranate seeds. Remove from heat and set aside to cool completely.

6. Pour sauce over panna cotta and serve immediately.

Pineapple and Yogurt Panna Cotta

I try to always have a batch of panna cotta in the fridge. My family loves it as a snack or a quick dessert. If I have impromptu visitors, I just dress it up with dried coconut or fruit syrup.

Tip

Always use canned or cooked pineapple when using gelatin. The bromelain enzyme in the raw fruit prevents gelatin from setting.

Make Ahead

This dessert can be prepared up to 2 days before and kept refrigerated.

- Six 8-ounce (250 mL) jars

6 tbsp	cold water	90 mL
4 tsp	unflavored gelatin powder	20 mL
2 cups	whole milk	500 mL
½ cup	granulated sugar	125 mL
1 tsp	vanilla extract	5 mL
2 cups	vanilla yogurt	500 mL
8	slices canned pineapple in syrup, drained and finely chopped	8

1. Place jars on a baking sheet and refrigerate for 30 minutes.

2. Pour water into a large bowl and sprinkle gelatin overtop. Set aside for 5 minutes.

3. In a saucepan, combine milk, sugar and vanilla extract. Heat over medium heat, stirring, until sugar dissolves completely. Pour over gelatin and whisk until gelatin is completely dissolved. Add yogurt and mix until well combined. Fold pineapple into yogurt mixture.

4. Spoon into jars, dividing equally. Refrigerate for at least 3 hours, until set, or for up to 2 days.

Vegetarian Gelatin

Gelatin powder is made from animal products. If you are a vegetarian, you will want to substitute an appropriate alternative. In my opinion the most suitable replacement is agar-agar, a colorless sea vegetable (seaweed) also known as kanten. It is available in natural foods stores and Asian markets. Unlike gelatin, agar-agar does not bloom in water. It needs to be stirred into hot liquid and come to a full boil for 3 to 5 minutes. If substituting agar-agar for gelatin in any recipe in this book, follow the manufacturer's instructions. Many brands of kosher gelatin (flavored or unflavored) are suitable for vegans — check the label and follow the manufacturer's instructions.

White Chocolate Panna Cotta with Liqueur

Makes 6 servings

This is one of the loveliest panna cottas I know. Adding a golden liqueur makes it elegant.

Tips

Use the best-quality white chocolate you can find.

Goldschläger liqueur is a cinnamon liqueur (schnapps) that contains fine gold flakes. Substitute an equal quantity of your favorite liqueur, anything from Kahlúa to Grand Marnier to Curaçao.

Make Ahead

The panna cotta can be prepared up to 2 days before and kept refrigerated.

- Six 8-ounce (250 mL) jars
- Small sieve

PANNA COTTA

6 tbsp	cold water	90 mL
4 tsp	unflavored gelatin powder	20 mL
4 cups	heavy or whipping (35%) cream	1 L
½ cup	granulated sugar	125 mL
1 tsp	vanilla extract	5 mL
½ cup	finely chopped white chocolate	125 mL

SAUCE

3 tbsp	apricot jam	45 mL
½ cup	Goldschläger liqueur (see Tips, left)	125 mL
3 tbsp	sliced almonds	45 mL

1. *Panna Cotta:* Place jars on a baking sheet and refrigerate for 30 minutes.

2. Pour water into a large bowl and sprinkle with gelatin overtop. Set aside for 5 minutes.

3. In a saucepan, combine cream, sugar and vanilla. Heat over low heat, stirring, until sugar dissolves completely. Add white chocolate and stir until melted. Pour mixture over the gelatin and whisk until gelatin is completely dissolved.

4. Place sieve over a jar and strain mixture into jar, filling to three-quarters. Repeat with remaining jars. Refrigerate for at least 6 hours, until set, or for up to 2 days.

5. *Sauce:* Just before serving, place apricot jam in a microwavable bowl and heat on High for 30 seconds. Stir and microwave again for 30 seconds. Remove from microwave and stir in liqueur. Drizzle over panna cotta, dividing equally. Sprinkle with almonds, dividing equally. Serve immediately.

Grapefruit and Mascarpone Panna Cotta

Here, refreshing grapefruit brings a lovely bite to rich mascarpone. Together they transform an effortless dessert into a tangy delicacy.

Tips

Use good-quality imported mascarpone for best results.

Try to find the best quality grapefruit marmalade, preferably one with low sugar content.

Make Ahead

The panna cotta can be prepared up to 2 days before and kept refrigerated.

- Eight 8-ounce (250 mL) jars

¼ cup	finely grated grapefruit zest	60 mL
¼ cup	freshly squeezed grapefruit juice	60 mL
4 tsp	unflavored gelatin powder	20 mL
2 cups	heavy or whipping (35%) cream	500 mL
½ cup	granulated sugar	125 mL
1	vanilla bean, cut lengthwise, seeds scraped out and reserved	1
2 cups	mascarpone cheese	500 mL
½ cup	grapefruit marmalade	125 mL

1. Place jars on a baking sheet and refrigerate for 30 minutes.

2. Pour grapefruit juice into a large bowl and sprinkle with gelatin. Set aside for 5 minutes.

3. In a saucepan, combine cream, sugar and vanilla pod and seeds. Set aside to infuse for 20 minutes. Place over medium heat and cook, stirring, until sugar dissolves completely. Remove from heat and remove and discard vanilla pod. Pour warm mixture over gelatin and whisk until gelatin is completely dissolved.

4. Place mascarpone and grapefruit zest in a large bowl. Slowly add cream mixture, whisking until well combined. Ladle mixture into jars, filling to three-quarters. Refrigerate for at least 4 hours, until set, or for up to 2 days.

5. When you're ready to serve, place grapefruit marmalade in a microwaveable bowl. Microwave on High for 30 seconds; stir and microwave again on High for 30 seconds. Stir and spoon over panna cotta, dividing equally. Serve immediately.

Blueberry, Lemon and Strawberry Panna Cotta with Vanilla Syrup

You will love serving panna cotta, for it is very easy to make. You can prepare it in advance and even bring it to picnics.

Tips

In the syrup, the vanilla extract may be substituted with 1 tsp (5 mL) cinnamon.

Lemon curd is the quintessential English treat, used for filling pies or cookies, for spreading on toast, etc. It can easily be found in supermarkets or fine food shops. The best-known brands are Robertson's, Crabtree and Evelyn, Gale's and Wilkin and Sons. It can be replaced by an equal quantity of prepared lemon pudding.

- Eight 8-ounce (250 mL) jars
- Fine-mesh sieve
- Blender

PANNA COTTA

1 cup	prepared lemon curd (see Tips, left)	250 mL
2 cups	sliced hulled strawberries	500 mL
1 cup	fresh or frozen blueberries	250 mL
2 cups	table (18%) cream	500 mL
6 tbsp	cold water	90 mL
5 tsp	unflavored gelatin powder	25 mL
2 cups	heavy or whipping (35%) cream	500 mL
1/2 cup	granulated sugar	125 mL
1	vanilla bean, split lengthwise, seeds scraped out and reserved	1
2 tsp	finely grated lemon zest	10 mL

SYRUP

1 cup	granulated sugar	250 mL
3/4 cup	water	175 mL
1 tbsp	vanilla extract	15 mL

1. *Panna Cotta:* Spoon lemon curd into jars, dividing equally. Place jars on a baking sheet and refrigerate for 30 minutes.

2. In blender, purée strawberries, blueberries and table cream. Place sieve over a bowl and pour mixture through. Discard solids. Set cream aside.

3. Place water in a large bowl and sprinkle with gelatin. Set aside for 5 minutes.

4. In a saucepan, combine fruit mixture, heavy cream, sugar and vanilla bean pod and seeds. Heat over medium heat, stirring, until sugar dissolves completely. Remove from heat. Remove and discard vanilla pod. Stir in lemon zest. Pour mixture over gelatin and whisk until gelatin is completely dissolved.

5. Carefully pour mixture into jars, filling to halfway. Refrigerate for at least 6 hours, until set, or up to 2 days.

The panna cotta can be prepared up to 2 days before and kept refrigerated.

The vanilla syrup can be prepared and kept refrigerated for up to 1 week.

6. *Syrup:* Meanwhile, in a saucepan, combine sugar and water. Bring to a boil over medium heat. Add vanilla, reduce heat and cook for 5 minutes, stirring. Remove from heat and set aside to cool completely. Refrigerate for at least 4 hours or up to 1 week.

7. When you're ready to serve, pour vanilla syrup over panna cotta, dividing equally, and serve immediately.

Vegetarian Gelatin

Gelatin powder is made from animal products. If you are a vegetarian, you will want to substitute an appropriate alternative. In my opinion the most suitable replacement is agar-agar, a colorless sea vegetable (seaweed) also known as kanten. It is available in natural foods stores and Asian markets. Unlike gelatin, agar-agar does not bloom in water. It needs to be stirred into hot liquid and come to a full boil for 3 to 5 minutes. If substituting agar-agar for gelatin in any recipe in this book, follow the manufacturer's instructions. Many brands of kosher gelatin (flavored or unflavored) are suitable for vegans — check the label and follow the manufacturer's instructions.

Trifles, Tiramisu and Chilled Cakes

White Chocolate and Coffee Trifle

Do you need an eye-opener dessert, one that's a real winner and a lifesaver when you have unexpected guests? Look no further — this is the one! Everyone will love it.

Tips

You can find good-quality prepared vanilla pudding in supermarkets. If you have leftover homemade pudding or custard, by all means use it in this recipe.

Coffee liqueur is a strongly flavored, sweet and intense alcoholic drink. It is made from roasted coffee beans and alcohol, and some have cream added. Make sure to use one that is good quality. The most popular — Kalhúa, Tia Maria, Starbucks, de Kuyper and Godiva — are used in many cocktails. If you do not want to use alcohol, it can be replaced by the same amount of cold, strong espresso coffee.

Do not refrigerate the trifle longer than 24 hours. It will become soggy.

- Six 8-ounce (250 mL) jars
- Electric mixer

PUDDING

2 cups	prepared vanilla pudding	500 mL
3 tbsp	instant espresso powder	45 mL

CREAM

1 cup	chopped white chocolate	250 mL
1 cup	heavy or whipping (35%) cream	250 mL
12	molasses cookies	12
¼ cup	coffee liqueur (see Tips, left)	60 mL

1. *Pudding:* In a bowl, combine vanilla pudding and espresso powder. Mix until coffee is completely incorporated. Set aside.

2. *Cream:* Place white chocolate in a microwavable bowl and microwave on High for 30 seconds. Remove from microwave and stir well, until evenly melted.

3. In a large bowl, using electric mixer at medium speed, whip cream to soft peaks. Slowly add melted white chocolate, whisking constantly. Continue whisking until cream is very thick. Set aside.

4. *Assembly:* Using a cookie cutter or the rim of a glass, cut molasses cookies into 12 rounds that will fit neatly inside your jars. Line bottoms of jars with 6 cookie rounds. (Trim to fit if needed.) Spoon coffee liqueur over cookies. Cover with half of the vanilla pudding and half of the white chocolate cream, dividing evenly. Repeat with remaining cookie rounds, pudding and cream. Cover and refrigerate for at least 30 minutes or up to 1 day before serving.

Variation

Milk Chocolate and Coffee Trifle: Substitute an equal quantity of milk chocolate for the white chocolate.

Mango Trifle

Trifle is the quintessential British dessert and it's easy to understand why — it delivers cake, custard and fruit all in one bite. This recipe captures the intense flavor of fragrant and delicious mangos.

Tips

You can purchase ready-made vanilla custard or make your own. Vanilla custard — also called crème anglaise — is available in cans (Ambrosia Devon Custard is a popular brand) or in the fresh dairy section of supermarkets. It is very practical to keep some on hand to make desserts or simply to pour over a brownie for an instant treat.

Try using Palmer mangoes when they're in season. They are picked ripe from the tree and as a result are less fibrous. They are also incredibly tasty.

- Eight 8-ounce (250 mL) straight-sided jars, buttered
- Electric mixer

MANGOS

3	mangos, peeled and diced	3
1/2 cup	granulated sugar	125 mL
1/4 cup	freshly squeezed lime juice	60 mL

CUSTARD

2 cups	prepared vanilla custard sauce (see Tips, left)	500 mL
2 tbsp	finely grated lime zest	30 mL

MANGO CREAM

1 cup	heavy or whipping (35%) cream	250 mL
1/2 cup	granulated sugar	125 mL
1/2 cup	mango nectar	125 mL

TOPPING

2 tbsp	packed brown sugar	30 mL
1 tbsp	finely grated lime zest	15 mL
4 cups	cubed (1/2 inch/1 cm) angel food cake, divided	1 L

1. *Mangos:* In a large bowl, toss mangos, sugar and lime juice. Cover and set aside at room temperature for 20 minutes.

2. *Custard:* In a bowl, whisk together custard sauce and lime zest. Set aside.

3. *Mango Cream:* In a large bowl, using electric mixer at medium speed, beat cream, sugar and mango nectar, until soft peaks form.

4. *Topping:* In a small bowl, mix brown sugar and lime zest. Set aside.

5. *Assembly:* Place 2 cups (500 mL) cake cubes in bottoms of jars, dividing equally. Press into place, using the bottom of a glass that will fit inside the jars. Cover with half of the custard mixture, dividing equally. In layers, add half of the whipped mango cream and mango cubes, dividing equally. Top with remaining cake (do not press down), dividing equally. In layers, add remaining custard, cream and fruit, dividing equally. Sprinkle with brown sugar mixture. Cover and refrigerate for 2 hours or up to 24 hours before serving.

Almond and Prune Trifle

Layers of prunes in cognac, rich custard cream and almonds — this recipe is a real treat in winter, when fresh fruits are not readily available. Serving it in a little jar or a pretty glass adds an element of fun to this dessert.

Tips

You can purchase ready-made vanilla custard or make your own. Vanilla custard — also called crème anglaise — is available in cans (Ambrosia Devon Custard is a popular brand) or in the fresh dairy section of supermarkets. It is very practical to keep some on hand to make desserts or simply to pour over a brownie for an instant treat.

Refrigerating trifle for at least 2 hours improves the result because the flavors can blend together and the cake soaks up the pudding. Yum!

Sponge cake is generally available in the bakery department of supermarkets. It can be replaced by pound cake.

- Eight 12-ounce (375 mL) jars
- Electric mixer

PRUNES

1 lb	dried pitted prunes (2 cups/500 mL)	500 g
1 cup	cognac	250 mL
1/2 cup	sliced almonds	125 mL

CREAM

1 cup	heavy or whipping (35%) cream	250 mL
1 cup	granulated sugar	250 mL
1/2 tsp	vanilla extract	2 mL

CUSTARD

2 cups	prepared vanilla custard sauce (see Tips, left)	500 mL
1/2 cup	almond flour	125 mL
4 cups	cubed (1/2 inch/1 cm) yellow sponge cake	1 L
1/2 cup	dark plum jam	125 mL

1. *Prunes:* In a deep dish, combine prunes and cognac. Cover and set aside for 1 hour. Drain, reserving liquid. Toss prunes with almonds. Set mixture aside.

2. *Cream:* In a large bowl, using electric mixer, whip cream, sugar and vanilla extract to soft peaks.

3. *Custard:* In a separate bowl, mix custard sauce and almond flour.

4. *Assembly:* Place 2 cups (500 mL) of the cake cubes in bottoms of jars, dividing equally. Drizzle with cognac marinade, dividing equally. Press into place, using the bottom of a glass that will fit inside the jars. Cover with half of the custard mixture, dividing equally. In layers, add half of the whipped cream and half of the prune mixture, dividing equally. Top with remaining cake (do not press down), dividing equally. In layers, add remaining custard, cream and fruit, dividing equally. Top each jar with a spoonful of plum jam. Cover and refrigerate for at least 2 hours or up to 8 hours before serving.

Lemon Trifle

Makes 6 servings

This dessert is the best solution for a fresh-tasting last course. It is rich and light at the same time. If you can find Meyer lemons, which are sweeter and less acidic than the usual kind, this will be one of the best lemon trifles you will ever make.

Tips

Lemon curd is the quintessential English treat, used for filling pies or cookies, for spreading on toast, etc. It can easily be found in supermarkets or fine food shops.

If you prefer, substitute an equal quantity of prepared lemon pie filling for the lemon curd.

If you have on hand leftover lemon cake, use it to replace the ladyfinger cookies. You will need about ³⁄₄ lb (375 g).

Make Ahead

This dessert can be made up to 2 days in advance.

- Six 12-ounce (375 mL) wide-mouth jars
- Electric mixer

LADYFINGERS

18	ladyfinger cookies, halved crosswise	18
1 cup	limoncello liqueur	250 mL

CREAM

1 cup	softened cream cheese	250 mL
2 cups	heavy or whipping (35%) cream	500 mL
¹⁄₂ cup	confectioner's (icing) sugar	125 mL
2 tbsp	finely grated lemon zest	30 mL
3 cups	lemon curd (see Tips, left)	750 mL

1. *Ladyfingers:* Place ladyfinger biscuits on a plate. Drizzle with limoncello liqueur, dividing equally. Set aside for 5 minutes.

2. *Cream:* In a large bowl, using electric mixer at medium speed, beat cream cheese until soft and very creamy. Add heavy cream and confectioner's sugar and beat until thick and creamy, about 6 minutes. Fold in lemon zest.

3. *Assembly:* Place 3 pieces of ladyfinger in the bottom of each jar. Top with half of the lemon curd and half of the whipped cream mixture, dividing equally. Repeat. Refrigerate overnight or for up to 2 days before serving.

Variation

If you prefer, when soaking the ladyfingers (Step 1), substitute ¹⁄₂ cup (125 mL) granulated sugar dissolved in 1 cup (250 mL) freshly squeezed lemon juice for the limoncello.

Rhubarb Trifle

When I was a little girl, my family, like most of our neighbors, always had rhubarb growing in the backyard. I used to cut off a stalk, peel it and eat it just like that. Of course, nothing could beat my grandmother's Sunday rhubarb trifle. I have my own version now and it always makes me think about how much I miss all that beautiful rhubarb growing in people's gardens. Adding orange zest to rhubarb preparations is a trick I learned from a great French chef. It works wonders.

Tips

Make your own waffles or use frozen ones, toasted.

Frozen rhubarb can be found all year round.

- Six 8-ounce (250 mL) straight-sided jars, buttered
- Sieve

CUSTARD

1/2 cup	granulated sugar	125 mL
1 1/4 cups	whole milk	300 mL
1 cup	heavy or whipping (35%) cream	250 mL
2	large egg yolks	2
3 tbsp	cornstarch	45 mL
Pinch	salt	Pinch
2 tbsp	unsalted butter, diced	30 mL
1 1/2 tsp	vanilla extract	7 mL

RHUBARB

1 1/2 lbs	rhubarb, trimmed and cut into 1-inch (2.5 cm) pieces (about 4 1/2 cups/1.125 L)	750 g
3/4 cup	granulated sugar	175 mL
2 tbsp	finely grated orange zest	30 mL
1/4 cup	freshly squeezed orange juice	60 mL

WAFFLES

8	cooked waffles, cut into small cubes (see Tips, left)	8
1/4 cup	cognac	60 mL
1/4 cup	thinly sliced almonds	60 mL

1. *Custard:* In a saucepan, whisk together sugar, milk, cream, egg yolks, cornstarch and salt. Cook over medium heat, whisking constantly, until thickened and bubbling, about 6 minutes. Pour through sieve into a large bowl. Stir in butter and vanilla, whisking until butter is incorporated. Press plastic wrap against the surface (to prevent a skin from forming) and refrigerate for at least 4 hours or up to 3 days.

2. *Rhubarb:* In a saucepan, combine rhubarb, sugar and orange zest and juice. Over medium heat, bring to a boil, stirring occasionally. Reduce heat and simmer, stirring often, until rhubarb has the texture of a thick compote, about 12 minutes. Remove from heat and set aside to cool completely.

Tip
You can refrigerate
this dessert for up to
4 hours, but if doing so,
cover with plastic.

3. *Waffles:* In a large bowl, combine waffle pieces and cognac. Press gently with fingertips to help them absorb the liquid.

4. *Assembly:* Spoon half of the waffle pieces into jars, dividing equally. Spoon half the custard over the waffles, then add half of the rhubarb compote, dividing equally. Repeat. Sprinkle with almonds and refrigerate for at least 1 hour (see Tip, left).

Double Tiramisu in a Jar

I was lucky enough to learn how to make this dessert from my friend Lorenza Biavaschi in Italy. But I perfected tiramisu after making it with the owner of the restaurant Trattoria da Giulio, in Lucca. I often ate there and never missed an opportunity to have a bowl of his tiramisu. It was absolutely the best in the world. And since what one has learned, one must share, here is his recipe.

Tips

Buy the best mascarpone and the best cocoa powder you can find and this simple dessert will be fantastic! And don't forget the coffee. People often tell me that they do not enjoy tiramisu. The taste of the coffee used to prepare it may be the cause.

Depending on the manufacturer, ladyfingers vary in size. Before soaking, cut them in half or into pieces that fit inside the jars. Place the pieces inside the jars to determine how many you'll need. You will need two layers in total.

- Six 8-ounce (250 mL) wide-mouth jars
- Electric mixer
- Fine-mesh sieve

MASCARPONE CREAM

2 cups	mascarpone cheese	500 mL
5	egg yolks	5
½ cup	granulated sugar	125 mL
4	egg whites	4
Pinch	salt	Pinch

LADYFINGERS

2 cups	strong coffee (preferably espresso)	500 mL
3 tbsp	Marsala wine, optional	45 mL
18	(approx.) ladyfingers (see Tips, left)	18
¼ cup	unsweetened cocoa powder	60 mL

1. *Mascarpone Cream:* In a large bowl, whisk together mascarpone, egg yolks and sugar until fluffy.

2. In another bowl, using electric mixer at high speed, whisk egg whites and salt until stiff peaks form. Using a metal spoon, very delicately fold egg whites into mascarpone mixture. Set aside.

3. *Ladyfingers:* In a shallow bowl, mix coffee and Marsala (if using). One by one, rapidly dip ladyfingers in the mixture (do not soak!).

4. *Assembly:* Cut ladyfingers in half (or into pieces that fit in the jars) and place side by side in a layer on the bottom of each jar (you want the bottoms to be completely covered). Cover with a thick layer of mascarpone cream. Add a thin layer of cocoa powder, dusted through the fine-mesh sieve. Cover with another layer of coffee-dipped ladyfingers. Cover with remaining mascarpone cream and finish with cocoa powder.

5. Refrigerate for at least 3 hours, or overnight for best results.

Raspberry and Mascarpone Tumbler

This is a very cute way to enjoy fresh raspberries and to extend the impact of just a few berries. Its incredible silkiness will convince you to make it again — and it's quickly prepared!

Tips

Use Triple Sec, Grand Marnier or Cointreau for the orange liqueur.

Raspberry syrup is available at specialty stores and well-stocked supermarkets. Teisseire, Torani and Monin are popular brands. If you prefer, replace the syrup with a coulis made from 1 cup (250 mL) crushed raspberries mixed with 1/2 cup (125 mL) granulated sugar and passed through a fine-mesh sieve.

You can use store-bought or homemade raspberry sorbet. Or, if you prefer, substitute an equal quantity of vanilla ice cream.

- Eight 8-ounce (250 mL) wide-mouth jars
- Electric mixer

MASCARPONE CREAM

2 cups	mascarpone cheese	500 mL
1/4 cup	confectioner's (icing) sugar	60 mL
1 tbsp	orange-flavored liqueur (see Tips, left)	15 mL
1 tsp	finely grated orange zest	5 mL
1 cup	heavy or whipping (35%) cream	250 mL
2 cups	fresh raspberries	500 mL

LADYFINGERS

1 cup	raspberry syrup (see Tips, left)	250 mL
20	ladyfingers, halved crosswise	20
8	small scoops raspberry sorbet, optional	8

1. *Mascarpone Cream:* In a bowl, using electric mixer at medium speed, beat mascarpone, confectioner's sugar, orange liqueur and orange zest until smooth. At high speed, slowly add cream, beating until fluffy and thick. Using a spatula, fold in raspberries. Set aside.

2. *Ladyfingers:* Pour raspberry syrup into a bowl. Quickly dip the ladyfinger pieces halfway into the syrup, just until they change color but are not softened by the liquid. Refrigerate remaining syrup. Place 5 soaked ladyfinger pieces upright in each jar, standing on cut ends around the perimeter of the glass (they may not cover the entire surface).

3. *Assembly:* Spoon mascarpone mixture into center of each jar (it will flow around the ladyfingers), dividing equally. Refrigerate for at least 30 minutes or up to 4 hours.

4. Top each glass with remaining raspberry syrup and a small scoop of raspberry sorbet (if using). Serve immediately.

Pumpkin Pecan Cheesecake

I made my best pumpkin desserts when I lived in Italy and France, where pumpkin as a dessert was not very popular. For the most part my friends had never tasted pumpkin pie before, but I made sure I also invited some American friends to vouch for me. Of course, at that time, cheesecake was not a big winner in French food circles either, because it was said to be *trop lourd* (too heavy). But this delicious combination won over even the most blasé French gourmands.

Tips

Homemade pumpkin purée can be frozen for up to 4 months. Thaw before using.

These cheesecakes can be prepared up to 2 days in advance up to the end of Step 5. Prepare the topping just before serving.

- Preheat oven to 325°F (160°C)
- Eight 8-ounce (250 mL) jars
- Fine-mesh sieve
- Electric mixer
- Baking pan large enough to accommodate the jars

CHEESECAKE

1½ cups	ricotta cheese	375 mL
1 cup	softened cream cheese	250 mL
4	eggs	4
½ cup	packed light brown sugar	125 mL
1½ cups	pumpkin purée (see Tip, page 179)	375 mL
¾ cup	buttermilk	175 mL
2 tbsp	cornstarch	30 mL
1 tsp	ground cinnamon	5 mL
1 tsp	ground ginger	5 mL
1 tsp	ground nutmeg	5 mL
1 cup	chopped pecans	250 mL
¼ tsp	ground black pepper	1 mL

TOPPING

½ cup	softened cream cheese	125 mL
½ cup	sour cream	125 mL
¼ cup	granulated sugar	60 mL
½ tsp	vanilla extract	2 mL

1. *Cheesecake:* Place sieve over a bowl and, using a wooden spoon, press ricotta through. Add cream cheese and, using electric mixer at medium speed, beat until smooth. Set aside.

2. In a large bowl, using electric mixer at medium speed, beat eggs and brown sugar until thick. Add pumpkin and beat at low speed until thoroughly combined.

3. In another bowl, whisk buttermilk, cornstarch, cinnamon, ginger and nutmeg. Add to strained ricotta and mix to combine. Add to pumpkin mixture and whisk to combine.

Tips

To make pumpkin purée from scratch, cut a ripe pie pumpkin in half, scoop out the seeds and stringy fibers, and lay face down on a baking sheet lined with parchment paper. Bake at 350°F (180°C) until soft, about 1½ hours. Cool, scoop out the flesh and purée in a food processor with 3 tbsp (45 mL) granulated sugar.

Making your own purée produces the best results, but in a pinch you can use canned purée. Just make sure it is pure pumpkin, not pumpkin pie filling, which has added ingredients.

4. Transfer to jars, dividing equally. Top with pecans (most will sink into the pudding). Sprinkle each jar with a pinch of black pepper.

5. Place jars in baking pan, spaced evenly apart and not touching the sides of the pan, and add enough hot water to come halfway up the sides of the jars. Transfer to preheated oven and bake for 40 minutes or until centers are just a bit wobbly. Remove from oven and set aside to cool completely.

6. *Topping:* In a bowl, using electric mixer at medium speed, beat cream cheese, sour cream, sugar and vanilla until soft and spreadable. Gently spread mixture over cooled pumpkin cheesecake. Serve immediately.

Black Forest Surprise

Sometimes the simplest ideas are the best. Chocolate cake, cherries and cream — the fundamentals of Black Forest cake, which has been an iconic German dessert since 1915, haven't changed. We may look for more exotic concoctions, but the only thing more exciting than an afternoon slice of Black Forest cake is enjoying it in a jar. This recipe uses marshmallow to give the dessert an even richer feel and provide a somewhat gooey experience. I strongly recommend trying it.

Tips

You will need a cookie cutter that is slightly smaller in circumference than the jars you are using, so the cake rounds will fit.

Use prepared marshmallow cream or make your own (see Tips, page 50).

If you prefer, substitute an equal quantity of whipped cream for the marshmallow cream.

- Eight 8-ounce (250 mL) jars
- Electric mixer
- Round cookie cutter or drinking glass (see Tips, left)

¾ cup	Kirsch	175 mL
3 tbsp	granulated sugar	45 mL
¼ cup	water	60 mL
1½ cups	pitted Bing cherries	375 mL
1½ cups	heavy or whipping (35%) cream	375 mL
2 tbsp	confectioner's (icing) sugar	30 mL
1 tsp	vanilla extract	5 mL
1	chocolate pound cake (fresh or frozen)	1
1½ cups	cherry pie filling	375 mL
1½ cups	marshmallow cream (see Tips, left)	375 mL
½ cup	chopped dark (70%) chocolate	125 mL

1. In a saucepan, combine Kirsch, sugar and water. Bring to a simmer, whisking to dissolve sugar. Set aside to cool.

2. Set aside 8 cherries to use as a garnish. Cut remainder in half. Set aside.

3. In a bowl, using electric mixer, whip cream, confectioner's sugar and vanilla until stiff peaks form. Set aside.

4. Slice pound cake into 16 thin slices. Using cookie cutter, cut 16 rounds to just fit inside the jars. Place one circle in each jar.

5. Pour 2 tsp (10 mL) Kirsch syrup over each cake circle. Cover with a layer of cherry pie filling and 1 tbsp (15 mL) marshmallow cream. Add a few fresh cherry halves. Cover with a thin layer of whipped cream. Add another layer of cake and remaining Kirsch syrup, cherry pie filling, marshmallow cream and halved cherries. Top with whipped cream.

6. Garnish with chopped chocolate and one whole cherry. Refrigerate for 2 hours before serving.

Goat Cheese and Fig Cheesecake

Weren't figs the fruits of the gods? If they weren't, they should have been. One of life's luxuries is picking your own fruits, and when I lived in Italy, I was fortunate enough to be able to pick my own figs. A little wrinkled and a little cracked from too much sun, these fruits were drunk with sweetness.

Tips

Always bring cream cheese and soft cheeses to room temperature so they can be mixed easily.

Use either green or black figs for this recipe.

Make Ahead

You can make these cheesecakes the day before and refrigerate until you're ready to serve.

- Preheat oven to 325°F (160°C), placing rack in middle position
- Eight 8-ounce (250 mL) wide-mouth jars, buttered
- Food processor
- Electric mixer
- Rimmed baking sheet, lined with parchment paper

CRUST

½ cup	crushed graham crackers	125 mL
¼ cup	melted unsalted butter	60 mL
¼ cup	ground almonds	60 mL
¼ cup	confectioner's (icing) sugar	60 mL

FILLING

1½ cups	softened cream cheese	375 mL
2 cups	fresh soft goat cheese	500 mL
5	large eggs	5
¾ cup	granulated sugar	175 mL
1 tbsp	finely grated lemon zest	15 mL
1 tsp	vanilla extract	5 mL
¼ cup	chopped walnuts	60 mL
8	fresh figs, cut into thin wedges, divided	8
4 tbsp	liquid honey	60 mL

1. *Crust:* In food processor, process graham crackers, melted butter, almonds and confectioner's sugar. Press into bottoms of jars and chill for 1 hour.

2. *Filling:* In a large bowl, using electric mixer at medium speed, beat cream cheese, goat cheese, eggs, sugar, lemon zest and vanilla until smooth. Fold in walnuts. Transfer filling to jars, dividing equally. Add half of one fig to each jar, pushing into the batter.

3. Place jars on baking sheet and bake in preheated oven for 35 minutes or until edges are set but centers are still wobbly. Remove from oven and set aside until cooled to room temperature.

4. When you're ready to serve, top with remaining figs and drizzle with honey, dividing equally.

From the Freezer

Chocolate and Orange Liqueur Iced Soufflé

A cross between chocolate mousse and ice cream, this incredibly delicate iced soufflé is a keeper for your personal recipe book.

Tips

Use any orange-flavored liqueur. Grand Marnier and Cointreau are my favorites.

If you have concerns about your egg supply and don't want to use raw eggs in a recipe, use pasteurized egg whites. Look at the package directions for the appropriate quantity to use.

- Six 8-ounce (250 mL) straight-sided jars, buttered
- Parchment paper
- Electric mixer

7 oz	dark (70%) chocolate, coarsely chopped	210 g
3½ oz	milk chocolate, coarsely chopped	100 g
3	egg yolks	3
¾ cup	granulated sugar	175 mL
½ cup	orange-flavored liqueur (see Tips, left)	125 mL
1½ cups	heavy or whipping (35%) cream	375 mL
3	egg whites (see Tips, left)	3
Pinch	salt	Pinch

1. Cut six strips of parchment paper, each long enough to fit securely around the exterior of a jar and extend 1 inch (2.5 cm) above the rim. Secure with rubber bands. Set jars aside.

2. Place dark and milk chocolate in a microwave-safe bowl. Heat on medium (50%) power for 3 minutes, stopping and stirring at one-minute increments. Remove from microwave and stir well, until melted and smooth.

3. In another bowl, using electric mixer at medium speed, beat egg yolks and sugar until pale and thick. Add orange liqueur and mix well. Fold in melted chocolate (it's okay to leave some streaks of chocolate in the mixture).

4. In another large bowl, using electric mixer with clean beaters at high speed, whip cream to stiff peaks. Fold into chocolate mixture.

5. In another large bowl, using electric mixer with clean beaters at high speed, beat egg whites and salt to stiff peaks. Fold very delicately into chocolate mixture. Carefully transfer to jars, spooning it to above the rim, all the way up to the top edge of the paper. Place in freezer overnight or for up to 3 days. Remove paper before serving.

Coffee Meringue Crunch

In my kitchen, as in most, there is always coffee. And because they keep for a long time, I always have a few meringues on hand to make impromptu desserts for unexpected guests. One Sunday afternoon, more friends than I had expected arrived, and that is when this dessert was created.

Tips

To soften the ice cream, place it in the refrigerator for 20 minutes.

You can buy meringue cookies or make your own (see recipe, page 97).

Make sure your walnuts are fresh (they tend to go rancid quickly). Refrigerate any that are left over for up to 1 month.

- Six 8-ounce (250 mL) jars

6	small meringue cookies (see Tips, left)	6
1/2 cup	chopped walnuts	125 mL
1/2 cup	shredded coconut	125 mL
1/2 cup	slivered almonds	125 mL
Pinch	nutmeg	Pinch
1 tbsp	instant espresso powder	15 mL
2 cups	softened coffee ice cream (see Tips, left)	500 mL

1. In a bowl, using a small knife, crush meringues into small pieces. Add walnuts, coconut, almonds, nutmeg and espresso powder and mix well. Fold in ice cream. Spoon into jars, dividing equally, and serve immediately.

Dulce de Leche and Apple Frozen Dessert

Dulce de leche is a variation on *confiture de lait*, or "milk jam." When the milk boils and its water content evaporates, it thickens and combines with sugar to create a deep caramel taste. It's a treat found in many countries, from Norway to South America, and no one is certain of its origin. One legend claims that Napoleon's cook got involved in a sudden battle and forgot the milk on the fire. When the skirmish ended, he served the sweet result to the soldiers.

Tip

You can also make dulce de leche from sweetened condensed milk. Simply pour 2 cans (14 oz/400 mL each) sweetened condensed milk into a large, microwave-safe bowl. Microwave on Medium (50% power) for 4 minutes, stirring twice. Reduce power to Low (30%) and cook for 10 minutes, whisking every few minutes, until thick and caramel-colored.

- Four 8-ounce (250 mL) jars
- Ice-cream scoop

DULCE DE LECHE

6 cups	whole milk	1.5 L
1½ cups	granulated sugar	375 mL
	Sea salt	
¾ tsp	baking soda	3 mL

CINNAMON SUGAR

½ cup	granulated sugar	125 mL
3 tbsp	ground cinnamon	45 mL
2 cups	apple sorbet	500 mL

1. *Dulce de Leche:* In a saucepan over medium heat, bring milk, sugar and salt to taste to a simmer. Remove from heat and whisk in baking soda (mixture will foam). Return to a simmer and cook over low heat, stirring often and skimming off foam, until sauce is golden brown and coats a spoon, about 45 minutes. Transfer to a large measuring cup. Pour half into jars, dividing equally. Set remainder aside.

2. *Cinnamon Sugar:* In a small bowl, mix sugar and cinnamon. Spread on a large plate.

3. Using ice-cream scoop, make 8 large balls of apple sorbet. Quickly roll each ball in cinnamon sugar. Place one ball in each jar. Top with remaining dulce de leche and a second apple sorbet ball. Serve immediately.

Banana Split in a Jar

One of the most decadent desserts I know. My daughter and I are guilty of enjoying several in the same evening while watching our favorite romantic movie.

Tips

If you have time, caramelize the bananas before using. Place slices on a baking sheet and sprinkle with 2 tbsp (30 mL) brown sugar. Place sheet under preheated broiler for 2 minutes. Transfer sheet to a wire rack and set aside to cool for 5 minutes before using. If you are caramelizing them, use unripe bananas, which won't soften too much.

Double the chocolate fudge sauce recipe, as it keeps for 1 week in the refrigerator. It is great for all kinds of desserts!

- Eight 8-ounce (250 mL) wide-mouth jars
- Electric mixer

FUDGE SAUCE

½ cup	packed brown sugar	125 mL
½ cup	unsweetened cocoa powder	125 mL
1 cup	evaporated milk	250 mL
¼ cup	corn syrup	60 mL
7 oz	chopped dark chocolate	210 g

ICE CREAM AND BANANAS

1 cup	heavy or whipping (35%) cream	250 mL
½ tsp	vanilla extract	2 mL
1 tbsp	granulated sugar	15 mL
3	bananas, peeled and sliced diagonally (see Tips, left)	3
1¼ cups	prepared strawberry sauce	300 mL
2 cups	vanilla ice cream or frozen yogurt	500 mL
¼ cup	chopped peanuts	60 mL
8	maraschino cherries	8

1. *Fudge Sauce:* In a saucepan, combine brown sugar, cocoa powder, evaporated milk and corn syrup. Over medium heat, stirring constantly, bring to a boil. Remove from heat and stir in chocolate until melted. Set aside.

2. *Ice Cream and Bananas:* In a bowl, using electric mixer at high speed, whip cream and vanilla to soft peaks. Gradually add granulated sugar, beating until thick. Set aside.

3. Working with one jar at a time, make a border of banana slices around the inside of the jar. Add a spoonful of strawberry sauce. Place a large scoop of vanilla ice cream in the center. Pour fudge sauce over ice cream. Top with chopped peanuts and a maraschino cherry. Repeat until all the jars are filled. Serve immediately.

Chocolate Pudding with Mint Sorbet

This recipe is certainly unusual, but it works! I use avocado for its buttery effect. The pudding is rich, creamy and quick to prepare.

Tips

Because this mint sorbet remains quite soft, after it has been frozen in the ice-cream maker it needs additional time in the freezer.

For a quick mint sorbet, purchase a good-quality lemon sorbet and process in a food processor with 3 cups (750 mL) chopped mint leaves. Freeze for at least 2 hours and use as directed.

- Six 8-ounce (250 mL) jars
- Ice-cream maker
- Food processor

MINT SORBET

2 cups	water	500 mL
2 cups	granulated sugar	500 mL
2 cups	packed chopped mint leaves	500 mL
1 tbsp	finely grated lemon zest	15 mL
1 cup	freshly squeezed lemon juice	250 mL

CHOCOLATE PUDDING

4	ripe avocados, peeled and diced	4
½ cup	liquid honey	125 mL
½ cup	unsweetened cocoa powder	125 mL
½ tsp	vanilla extract	2 mL
Pinch	salt	Pinch

1. *Mint Sorbet:* In a saucepan over medium heat, combine water, sugar and mint. Bring to a boil and cook, stirring often, until sugar is completely dissolved. Cover, remove from heat and set aside for 15 minutes to steep. Stir in lemon zest and juice. Refrigerate for 2 hours, until chilled.

2. Transfer to ice-cream maker and freeze according to manufacturer's instructions. Transfer to a container and place in the freezer for at least 4 hours or up to 2 days before serving (see Tips, left).

3. *Chocolate Pudding:* In food processor, pulse avocados, honey, cocoa and vanilla for 1 minute. Add salt and process until smooth. Transfer to jars, dividing equally. Refrigerate for at least 2 hours or up to 1 day. When you're ready to serve, scoop mint sorbet over chocolate pudding and serve immediately.

Frozen Cookies and Cream

Only for children, you say? My mother (who would kill me if I revealed her age) cannot resist one of these frozen delights. To please the entire family, you can triple the recipe.

Tip

Traditional Oreo cookies can be used, or any other cream-filled favorites.

- Four 8-ounce (250 mL) individual jars
- Electric mixer

12	cream-filled cookies, divided (see Tip, left)	12
2 cups	heavy or whipping (35%) cream	500 mL
½ cup	granulated sugar	125 mL
½ tsp	vanilla extract	2 mL
½ cup	sour cream	125 mL
4 tbsp	chocolate syrup	60 mL

1. Place one cookie in the bottom of each jar. Break remaining cookies into small pieces and set aside.

2. In a bowl, using electric mixer at high speed, beat cream, sugar and vanilla to soft peaks. Add sour cream and beat until stiff peaks form. Fold in crushed cookies. Spoon into jars. Cover and freeze for at least 2 hours or up to 3 days.

3. When you're ready to serve, place jars in the refrigerator for 20 minutes to soften. Top with chocolate syrup.

Brownie Frozen Delight

Is there anything more comforting than a brownie? Sometimes I get carried away and make so many that I have lots of extra brownies. That's good news, because I can use them to make this delight. This is my family's favorite leftovers recipe.

Tips

To soften the ice cream, place it in the refrigerator for 1 hour.

The results are even better if your brownies are a few days old.

• Eight 8-ounce (250 mL) wide-mouth jars, buttered

½ cup	heavy or whipping (35%) cream	125 mL
1 cup	chopped pecans	250 mL
½ cup	chocolate chips	125 mL
2 cups	softened vanilla ice cream (see Tips, left)	500 mL
4	brownies (each about 2 inches/5 cm square), cut in small pieces, divided	4
½ cup	prepared caramel sauce	125 mL
1 tsp	fleur de sel	5 mL
½ cup	raspberries, optional	125 mL

1. In a bowl, using an electric mixer at high speed, whip cream to soft peaks. Fold in pecans and chocolate chips.

2. Place softened ice cream in a large bowl. Add whipped cream mixture and fold in gently.

3. Transfer to jars, filling each one-third full. Add half the brownie pieces to jars, dividing equally. Drizzle a few drops of caramel sauce into each jar and sprinkle with a few grains of fleur de sel. Mix raspberries (if using) into remaining ice cream mixture. Spoon into jars, dividing equally. Cover and freeze for at least 2 hours or up to 4 days.

4. When you are ready to serve, add the remaining brownie pieces.

Variation

Substitute an equal quantity of chocolate ice cream for the vanilla.

Peaches and Cream Pudding

When peaches come into season, it is a reminder that the summer is going by too fast. This is one of my favorite late-summer desserts because every bite contains a tasty surprise.

Tip

To soften the ice cream for this recipe, place in the refrigerator for 30 minutes.

- Eight 8-ounce (250 mL) jars
- Round cookie cutter, slightly smaller than diameter of jars
- Electric mixer

2 cups	softened vanilla ice cream (see Tip, left)	500 mL
8	ripe peaches, peeled and diced	8
8	store-bought individual sponge cakes	8
2 cups	heavy or whipping (35%) cream	500 mL
½ cup	granulated sugar	125 mL
2 cups	peach sorbet	500 mL

1. Place ice cream in a large bowl. Using a spatula, fold in peaches. Pour into a wide, deep dish. Cover with plastic wrap and place in freezer for 1 hour.

2. Place one sponge cake in bottom of each jar, cutting to fit if necessary.

3. Remove ice cream from freezer. Using cookie cutter, cut out 8 rounds and place in jars. Refrigerate.

4. In a large bowl, using electric mixer at medium speed, beat cream and sugar to stiff peaks.

5. Place a scoop of peach sorbet in each jar. Top with whipped cream, dividing equally, and serve immediately.

Sweet Soups, Parfaits, Frothy Desserts and So On

Cold Cantaloupe Soup with Mint

With its musky aroma and warm flavors, a cantaloupe is full of surprises. If the sign of a good cook is making simple things well, this is an easy recipe to prove that theory. Although appropriate for an elegant dinner, this soup will be a hit at any meal. Sometimes I like to take it to picnics, in jars set on ice.

Tips

Choose strongly scented cantaloupes and do not refrigerate them before making this recipe. In summer, watch for cantaloupes that are a bit cracked — they are usually the sweetest.

Be generous with the pepper, for it enhances the flavor of cantaloupes.

Make Ahead

This recipe can be prepared up to 8 hours before serving. Make sure to wrap both the melon balls and the soup in a double layer of plastic wrap before refrigerating. Cantaloupe has a pungent smell that tends to permeate other foods in the fridge.

- Eight 8-ounce (250 mL) jars, chilled

4	small cantaloupes, halved, seeds removed and discarded, divided	4
4 tbsp	granulated sugar, divided	60 mL
1	small bunch fresh mint, leaves only, divided	1
1 cup	dry white wine	250 mL
1 tsp	freshly ground black pepper	5 mL
1 tsp	finely grated orange zest	5 mL
1 tsp	finely grated lime zest	5 mL
1 cup	hulled small strawberries	250 mL
1 tbsp	port wine	15 mL

1. Using a melon baller (or a small spoon) and 2 of the cantaloupe halves, make cantaloupe balls. Transfer to a bowl and sprinkle with 1 tbsp (15 mL) sugar. Cover and refrigerate.

2. Scoop out flesh of remaining cantaloupes and transfer to a blender. Add 12 mint leaves and purée. Add remaining sugar and pulse to blend. Add white wine, pepper, orange and lime zest and 8 mint leaves. Pulse to blend. Transfer to a large bowl and chill for at least 3 hours or up to 8 hours.

3. When you are ready to serve, spoon cantaloupe balls into jars, dividing equally. Add chilled soup, dividing equally. Add a few strawberries to each jar, dividing equally, and garnish with a few mint leaves. Finish with a dash of port wine and serve immediately.

Variation

This recipe can be made using the same quantity of honeydew melons. Replace the port wine with a dash of vodka.

Cold Strawberry Orange Soup

This recipe is a real winner — quick, easy and delicious. As a summer dessert that virtually everyone (even those who are watching their waistlines) can enjoy, it is perfect. And it is so satisfying that no one will think it's a "light" dessert.

Tips

Use a funnel to pour this soup neatly into the jars without making a mess.

If you like this soup as much as I do, make it all year long, using frozen strawberries.

- Six 8-ounce (250 mL) jars
- Food processor or blender

4 cups	hulled fresh strawberries	1 L
½ cup	confectioner's (icing) sugar	125 mL
1 cup	orange juice	250 mL
3 tbsp	chopped fresh mint leaves, divided	45 mL
1 tbsp	finely grated orange zest	15 mL
1 tsp	granulated sugar	5 mL
1 tbsp	slivered almonds	15 mL
¼ cup	plain yogurt	60 mL
6	mint leaves	6

1. In food processor fitted with the metal blade, purée strawberries. Add confectioner's sugar and process for 1 minute. Add orange juice and process for 1 minute. Add 1 tbsp (15 mL) mint and process for 1 minute. Transfer to jars, dividing equally, and refrigerate for 1 hour.

2. In a bowl, mix remaining mint, orange zest, granulated sugar and almonds. Add yogurt and mix well. Top each jar with a dollop (about 1 tbsp/15 mL) of the mixture, garnish with a mint leaf and serve immediately.

Rhubarb and Strawberry Parfait

Makes 6 servings

Tart rhubarb is often paired with strawberries to add sweetness and give it a ruby-red color. Rhubarb is not used as much as it was in the past, but it should be brought back more often, because it really stimulates the taste buds.

Tips

Orange-flavored liqueurs include Triple Sec, Grand Marnier and Cointreau.

Avoid buying floppy soft rhubarb. Look for crisp, stiff stalks to ensure its freshness.

Make Ahead

The rhubarb compote can be made up to 3 days ahead.

- Six 12-ounce (375 mL) jars
- Blender
- Electric mixer

RHUBARB

3 cups	chopped rhubarb	750 mL
1 cup	granulated sugar	250 mL
¼ cup	freshly squeezed orange juice	60 mL

STRAWBERRIES

2 cups	halved hulled strawberries	500 g
¼ cup	orange-flavored liqueur (see Tips, left)	60 mL
2 tbsp	confectioner's (icing) sugar	30 mL
2 cups	heavy or whipping (35%) cream	500 mL
2 tbsp	finely grated lemon zest	30 mL

1. *Rhubarb:* In a saucepan over medium heat, bring rhubarb, sugar and orange juice to a boil. Reduce heat and simmer until rhubarb is tender, stirring often. Remove from heat and set aside to cool for 15 minutes.

2. Transfer cooled mixture to blender and blend at high speed until smooth. Transfer to a bowl, cover and refrigerate for at least 1 hour or up to 3 days.

3. *Strawberries:* In a bowl, combine strawberries, orange liqueur and confectioner's sugar. Cover and set aside for 10 minutes.

4. In a bowl, using electric mixer at high speed, beat cream until soft peaks form. Fold in lemon zest. Fold whipped cream into rhubarb mixture.

5. *Assembly:* Spoon half the rhubarb cream into jars, dividing equally. Using a slotted spoon, add half the strawberries. Repeat. Top each jar with 1 tsp (5 mL) strawberry juices. Serve immediately.

Variations

Rhubarb and Raspberry Parfait: Substitute an equal quantity of raspberries for the strawberries.

Rhubarb Orange Parfait: Substitute an equal quantity of orange segments for the strawberries. An original partnership, rhubarb plus oranges provides an intense and unforgettable taste.

Mango Parfait

Makes 4 servings

One of the most popular exotic fruits, the mango here brings its tangy flavor to a perfect companion — yogurt. This is my family's favorite healthy treat after lunch.

Tips

For a sweeter treat, add 1 tbsp (15 mL) maple syrup to the top of each jar. Mango and maple syrup are a great match.

Since different types of mangoes will have more or less flesh, adjust the quantity to suit. Use any leftover mango purée to make a smoothie for the cook.

- Four 8-ounce (250 mL) tall jars
- Food processor

MANGOS

3	mangos, peeled and sliced, divided	3
2 tbsp	granulated sugar	30 mL
½ tsp	ground cardamom	2 mL
2 cups	Greek-style vanilla yogurt	500 mL

1. *Mangos:* In food processor fitted with the metal blade, purée the flesh of 2 mangos with the sugar.

2. Place remaining mango slices in a bowl. Sprinkle with cardamom and mix gently. Set aside.

3. *Assembly:* Spoon approximately 2 tbsp (30 mL) mango purée into the bottom of each jar. Cover with ¼ cup (60 mL) vanilla yogurt. Repeat. When ready to serve, garnish with reserved mango slices.

Peach and Mango Parfait

Two of everyone's favorite fruits in one scoop, plus a dash of maple syrup to sweeten. Not only is this dessert delicious, it is especially easy to prepare.

Tips

For better results, use pure maple syrup. Maple-flavored and other artificially flavored syrups should be avoided because they have none of the benefits of real maple syrup and they contain too much sugar. Pure maple syrup is actually a healthy sweetener. It provides manganese, zinc, potassium and riboflavin, among other nutrients.

You can purchase canned mango purée at most supermarkets. You can also make your own. To produce the quantity required for this recipe, purée 4 large mangoes (you may need a bit more or less, depending on the variety), ¼ cup (60 mL) granulated sugar and 1 tbsp (15 mL) freshly squeezed lemon juice.

• Six 8-ounce (250 mL) tall jars

PEACHES

| 4 | peaches, peeled and sliced | 4 |
| ½ cup | maple syrup | 125 mL |

MANGO PURÉE

3 cups	plain yogurt	750 mL
2 cups	mango purée (see Tips, left)	500 mL
2 tbsp	sliced almonds	30 mL

1. *Peaches:* In a bowl, combine peaches and maple syrup.

2. *Mango Purée:* In another bowl, whisk together yogurt and mango purée. Fold in almonds.

3. *Assembly:* Spoon half the mango mixture into jars, dividing equally. Cover with peach mixture, dividing equally. Top with the rest of the mango mixture and serve immediately.

Peanut Butter Parfait

Peanut butter is much more than something you spread on toast. It also loves being made into a dessert. As always, it makes a perfect duo with chocolate.

Tip

For best results, use "natural" peanut butter, which does not contain added unhealthy fats. Read the label: peanuts and salt should be the only ingredients. It will tend to separate in the jar; just stir before using.

- Four 8-ounce (250 mL) jars
- Electric mixer
- Food processor

PEANUT BUTTER

1 cup	heavy or whipping (35%) cream	250 mL
2 tbsp	confectioner's (icing) sugar	30 mL
1/2 cup	smooth peanut butter	125 mL

ICE CREAM

2 cups	chocolate ice cream, softened for 15 minutes in refrigerator	500 mL
1/2 cup	sour cream	125 mL
2 tbsp	chopped roasted, unsalted peanuts	30 mL

1. *Peanut Butter:* In a bowl, using electric mixer at high speed, whip cream and confectioner's sugar to stiff peaks.

2. In another bowl, beat peanut butter until very smooth. Fold in whipped cream. Pour half the mixture into jars, dividing equally.

3. *Ice Cream:* In food processor fitted with the metal blade, pulse ice cream and sour cream until blended.

4. *Assembly:* Carefully spoon ice cream mixture into jars, dividing equally. Cover with remaining peanut butter cream, dividing equally. Freeze for 30 minutes. Top with chopped peanuts and serve.

Mascarcino

Makes 8 servings

In this recipe, the light, frothy topping balances the rich and creamy filling. Made with mascarpone and a cappuccino-like topping, this simple dessert is a lovely way to end a friendly get-together.

Tips

Make sure to use instant espresso powder. Other instant coffees will not deliver the appropriate flavor.

To melt chocolate: Place chopped chocolate in a bowl over a saucepan half-filled with boiling water (the bowl should not touch the water). Melt chocolate over low heat, stirring constantly. You can also melt chocolate in the microwave. Place chopped chocolate in a microwave-safe bowl and heat on Low for about 1 minute per ounce (30 g), stirring after each minute. Whether you use the microwave or stovetop method, make sure that not even a drop of water comes in contact with the chocolate; that will cause it to "seize," or form hard clumps.

- Eight 8-ounce (250 mL) jars, buttered
- Electric mixer
- Immersion blender, optional

MASCARPONE CREAM

2 cups	mascarpone cheese	500 mL
2 tbsp	granulated sugar	30 mL
¼ cup	instant espresso powder (see Tips, left)	60 mL
1 cup	melted dark or bittersweet chocolate (see Tips, left)	250 mL

TOPPING

2 cups	2% milk	500 mL
1 tsp	unsweetened cocoa powder	5 mL

1. *Mascarpone Cream:* In a bowl, using electric mixer at medium speed, beat mascarpone and sugar for 2 minutes. Add espresso powder and melted chocolate and beat until incorporated. Spoon into jars, dividing equally. Refrigerate for at least 30 minutes or up to 2 days.

2. *Topping:* When you're ready to serve, heat milk in a saucepan (do not boil). Using an immersion blender, process until thick foam forms on top. Place a large spoonful of milk foam on top of each mascarpone cream. (If you have a cappuccino machine, use the frother to prepare the milk.) Sprinkle with cocoa powder and serve immediately.

Pink Chantilly with Cranberries

Filled with antioxidants and loaded with vitamin C, cranberries are very healthful. However, we hear so much about their health benefits that we sometimes forget how truly delicious they can be. This recipe is certainly the simplest and one of the most beautiful ways to serve cranberries.

Tips

Make sure to use real maple syrup. Maple-flavored and other table syrups contain a lot of granulated sugar or corn syrup and do not cook the same way. It's worth every penny to get the real thing.

Make this recipe just before dinner for a quick and happy treat.

- Four 8-ounce (250 mL) tall jars
- Blender
- Fine-mesh sieve
- Electric mixer

1½ cups	raspberries, fresh or frozen	375 mL
3 tbsp	confectioner's (icing) sugar	45 mL
2 cups	frozen cranberries, thawed	500 mL
½ cup	maple syrup (see Tips, left)	250 mL
1½ cups	heavy or whipping (35%) cream	375 mL
1 tbsp	granulated sugar	15 mL
1 tsp	vanilla extract	5 mL
½ cup	cranberry juice	125 mL
	Mint leaves	

1. In blender, purée raspberries and confectioner's sugar. Transfer to a fine-mesh sieve placed over a bowl and press mixture through. Discard seeds and set raspberry purée aside.

2. In a saucepan over medium heat, cook cranberries and maple syrup, stirring often, for 15 minutes. Remove from heat and set aside to cool.

3. In a large bowl, using electric mixer at high speed, whip cream, granulated sugar and vanilla until soft peaks begin to form. Beating constantly, slowly add cranberry juice and half the raspberry purée.

4. Spoon remaining raspberry purée into jars, dividing equally. Top with whipped cream mixture, dividing equally. Refrigerate for up to 30 minutes.

5. When you're ready to serve, remove jars from refrigerator and top with cooked cranberries. Using a long spoon, mix delicately. Garnish with mint leaves and serve immediately.

Variations

Raspberry Chantilly: Substitute an equal quantity of frozen raspberries for the cranberries.

Blueberry Chantilly with Cranberries: Substitute an equal quantity of frozen blueberries for the raspberries.

Raspberry and Coconut Fool

Elegance is often found in the simplest of things. I love fools, which are basically crushed fruit or berries mixed with whipped cream. They are so easy to prepare and yet everyone wants more.

Tips

Use fresh or frozen raspberries to prepare the cream. If using frozen, I recommend having 1 cup (250 mL) fresh raspberries on hand for adding to the jars.

Double the quantity and freeze for up to 4 days for a terrific frozen treat.

Make Ahead

This recipe can be prepared up to 3 hours ahead and kept refrigerated.

- Four 8-ounce (250 mL) jars or six 6-ounce (175 mL) tumblers
- Food processor or blender
- Fine-mesh sieve
- Electric mixer

3 cups	raspberries, divided	750 mL
1 cup	coconut cream	250 mL
¾ cup	heavy or whipping (35%) cream	175 mL
¼ cup	granulated sugar	60 mL
¼ cup	coconut or raspberry liqueur	60 mL

1. In food processor fitted with the metal blade, purée 2 cups (500 mL) raspberries. Using a rubber spatula, press through sieve set over a bowl; discard seeds. Return purée to food processor. Add coconut cream and process for 2 minutes. Set aside.

2. In a bowl, using electric mixer at high speed, whip cream and sugar until stiff peaks form. Gently fold in raspberry-coconut purée. Spoon into jars, dividing equally. Add remaining whole raspberries and push into cream. Cover and refrigerate for at least 30 minutes or up to 3 hours before serving.

3. Top each jar with liqueur, dividing equally, and serve immediately.

Cherry Berry Smoothie

Makes 3 to 4 servings

This has to be the best creamy cherry dessert you'll ever enjoy. Be aware, the yield will vary depending on the berries used. You may get three very generous servings or four that don't quite reach the tops of the jars. I like to serve this in "drinking jars."

Tips

Substitute an equal quantity of low-fat milk for the almond milk.

Ground almonds are often called "almond flour." They are available in well-stocked supermarkets or natural foods stores.

- Four 12-ounce (375 mL) tall jars
- Blender

1 cup	frozen mixed berries	250 mL
1 cup	frozen pitted cherries	250 mL
1	ripe banana, peeled	1
1 cup	cherry-flavored yogurt	250 mL
½ cup	almond milk (see Tips, left)	125 mL
2 tbsp	liquid honey	30 mL
2 tbsp	plain yogurt	30 mL
2 tbsp	ground almonds (see Tips, left)	30 mL

1. In blender, purée berries, cherries, banana, cherry yogurt, almond milk and honey. Blend at high speed for 2 minutes. Pour into jars, dividing equally.

2. In a bowl, mix plain yogurt and almonds. Top each jar with a dollop of the mixture and serve immediately.

Orange and Cognac Syllabub

Syllabub, a frothy liquid dessert that originated in England in the sixteenth century, makes a wonderful warm-weather treat. This one is very quick to make but oh, so decadent! The wonderful scent of orange brings a fresh touch to this down-to-earth sweet. Serve it with wafers or other simple cookies.

Tip

Sweet wines such as French Vouvray or Sauternes or Italian Passito di Pantelleria work well in this dessert. If you prefer, substitute an equal quantity of ice cider (also called apple ice wine) for an equally delicious result.

- Four 8-ounce (250 mL) tall jars
- Electric mixer

½ cup	cognac	125 mL
¼ cup	sweet white wine (see Tip, left)	60 mL
2 tbsp	finely grated orange zest	30 mL
½ cup	freshly squeezed orange juice	125 mL
¼ cup	granulated sugar	60 mL
2 cups	heavy or whipping (35%) cream	500 mL
Pinch	nutmeg	Pinch
	Wafers	

1. In a large bowl, mix cognac, wine, orange zest and juice and sugar.

2. In a bowl, using electric mixer at high speed, beat cream and nutmeg to soft peaks. Beating constantly, slowly add cognac mixture; beat until cream just begins to form stiff peaks.

3. Spoon mixture into jars and refrigerate for up to 1 hour. Serve with wafers.

Maple Syrup Syllabub

Syllabub is one of those ancient desserts that never grow old. Quick and easy, it is perfect for entertaining. It is an ideal way to finish a large meal and can be prepared several hours before serving. I served this North American version of a traditional syllabub at a bridal party as an extra to the official dessert, and it was a great success.

Tips

Dark maple syrup has a very strong flavor, which I like in this recipe. However, if you don't have it, use amber or even medium maple syrup.

Sweet wines such as French Vouvray or Sauternes can be used in this recipe, but they tend to be expensive. Try ice cider (apple ice wine) for a nice crisp flavor.

- Six 8-ounce (250 mL) tall jars
- Electric mixer

1/2 cup	dark maple syrup (see Tips, left)	125 mL
1/4 cup	maple sugar	60 mL
2 tbsp	sweet white wine (see Tips, left)	30 mL
1 tbsp	finely grated orange zest	15 mL
2 cups	heavy or whipping (35%) cream	500 mL
2 cups	softened maple ice cream	500 mL
1 tsp	ground nutmeg	5 mL

1. In a bowl, combine maple syrup, maple sugar, wine and orange zest. Mix well, cover and set aside for 30 minutes.

2. In a large bowl, using electric mixer at high speed, whip cream until soft peaks form. Slowly pour in maple mixture, beating until peaks form.

3. Place a small scoop of maple ice cream in each jar. Top with cream mixture, dividing equally. Sprinkle with nutmeg and serve immediately.

Maple Rosemary Syllabub

Sophisticated yet simple to prepare, syllabub is usually made with cream and wine or an aromatic liqueur whipped into froth. It was once so popular that there were special syllabub glasses, with two handles, a cover and a spout. In this modern version the delicate touch of maple is paired with cream.

Tips

Maple sugar is a delicate sweet made from the sap of sugar maple trees. It is available in specialty stores in granulated form or pressed into a solid block, which needs to be grated. If you can't find it, substitute granulated sugar, using 1 tsp (5 mL) less.

Maple liqueur is made in Vermont and in Canada. It is available at fine liquor stores. If you don't have it, substitute 1 part whisky and 2 parts pure maple syrup.

Be careful not to overwhip after adding the liquid ingredients. Otherwise the mixture will become grainy.

- Four 8-ounce (250 mL) jars, chilled for 30 minutes
- Electric mixer

1 cup	heavy or whipping (35%) cream	250 mL
1/4 cup	maple sugar (see Tips, left)	60 mL
1/4 tsp	ground nutmeg	1 mL
1 cup	pure maple syrup	250 mL
1/2 cup	sweet white wine	125 mL
1/4 cup	maple liqueur (see Tips, left)	60 mL
1/2 tsp	finely grated lemon zest	2 mL
4	sprigs rosemary	4

1. In a large bowl, using electric mixer at high speed, beat cream, maple sugar and nutmeg until soft peaks form. Beating constantly, add maple syrup and continue beating until peaks form. Slowly add wine and maple liqueur and continue beating until just thick. Using a spatula, fold in lemon zest. Transfer to jars, dividing equally, and refrigerate for at least 30 minutes or up to 2 hours.

2. When you're ready to serve, garnish each jar with a sprig of rosemary.

Hogmanay Syllabub with Whisky

Are you planning a trip to Scotland? You should know the Scots have a rich heritage associated with New Year's Eve, and they have their own name for it — Hogmanay. This is a recipe for a special syllabub that is perfect for the holidays. I add a dash of ginger, since it goes so well with whisky. Surprise your guests!

Tip

The quality of the whisky used in this recipe will make a big difference to connoisseurs.

- Six 8-ounce (250 mL) tall jars
- Electric mixer

¼ cup	quick-cooking oatmeal	60 mL
¼ cup	whisky, preferably Scotch (see Tip, left)	60 mL
2 tbsp	freshly squeezed lemon juice	30 mL
2 cups	heavy or whipping (35%) cream	500 mL
3 tbsp	cold milk	45 mL
⅛ tsp	ground ginger	0.5 mL
2 tbsp	grated dark (64%) chocolate	30 mL

1. In a saucepan, combine oatmeal, whisky and lemon juice. Stir and set aside for 5 minutes to soak. Place on stovetop over low heat and cook until thickened, about 7 minutes. Remove from heat and set aside to cool completely.

2. In a large bowl, using electric mixer at high speed, whip cream until soft peaks form. Slowly fold in oatmeal mixture and milk. Fold in ginger and grated chocolate. Transfer to jars, dividing equally, and serve immediately.

Iced Mocha Syllabub

For coffee lovers, this is the ultimate dessert with a punch.

Tips

Use homemade or the best-quality coffee ice cream for this recipe. To soften, place in the refrigerator for about 20 minutes.

Do not substitute regular instant coffee for the espresso powder, because instant coffee does not have the same rich, aromatic flavor. Instant coffee would result in a bitter taste.

- Four 8-ounce (250 mL) tall jars, buttered
- Blender
- Electric mixer

3¼ oz	dark chocolate (70%), melted	100 g
¼ cup	granulated sugar	60 mL
2 tbsp	instant espresso powder (see Tips, left)	30 mL
½ tsp	vanilla extract	2 mL
Pinch	nutmeg	Pinch
½ cup	brandy	125 mL
½ cup	mascarpone cheese	125 mL
2 cups	heavy or whipping (35%) cream	500 mL
2 cups	softened coffee ice cream (see Tips, left)	500 mL
1 tbsp	unsweetened cocoa powder	15 mL

1. In blender, process melted chocolate, sugar, espresso powder, vanilla, nutmeg and brandy until smooth.

2. In a large bowl, using electric mixer at medium speed, beat mascarpone for 2 minutes, until creamy. Add cream and beat until stiff peaks form. Gradually add chocolate mixture, beating constantly. Fold in softened ice cream.

3. Spoon into jars and refrigerate for 30 minutes. When you're ready to serve, dust each jar with cocoa powder, dividing equally.

Pear and Chocolate Frosty

This is an extra-quick dessert recipe that is perfect for children or teenagers to make. When she was at university, I equipped my daughter with only two electric gadgets: a toaster (for peanut butter sandwiches) and a blender, so she could make this delicious dessert, which requires few ingredients, no particular culinary talent and no time. The best part is that it's delicious.

Tip

Try to find dark chocolate milk. It is richer and tastier than regular chocolate milk.

- Four 12-ounce (375 mL) tall jars
- Blender

8	canned pear halves in syrup, divided	8
4 cups	cold chocolate milk	1 L
2 cups	cold sweetened condensed milk	500 mL
1 cup	ice cubes	250 mL

1. Cut 3 of the pear halves into cubes. Transfer to jars, dividing equally.

2. In blender, purée remaining pears and $\frac{1}{4}$ cup (60 mL) of their syrup. Add chocolate milk, condensed milk and ice cubes. Pulse until the ice cubes are crushed, then blend for 1 minute.

3. Pour over cubed pears, dividing equally. Refrigerate for 30 minutes before serving.

Variation

If you prefer, purée all the pears in the blender and serve this dessert in a drinking jar as a milkshake dessert.

Coconut Granita with Licorice Sauce

This recipe combines two exotic tastes. It may seem strange, but the rich flavor of coconut and the refreshing taste of licorice are a terrific match.

Tip

Shredded coconut is moist and generally sweetened. Unopened, a bag will keep for several months at room temperature. Once opened, keep leftover coconut in the refrigerator for up to 2 months.

- Four 8-ounce (250 mL) jars

GRANITA

2 cups	whole milk	500 mL
1 cup	coconut milk	250 mL
1 cup	shredded coconut (see Tips, left)	250 mL
¼ cup	granulated sugar	60 mL
1 tbsp	finely grated lime zest	15 mL

LICORICE SAUCE

½ cup	store-bought caramel sauce	125 mL
½ cup	heavy or whipping (35%) cream	125 mL
12	black licorice jellybeans	12
1 tsp	aniseed	5 mL

1. *Granita:* Place a large, shallow plastic container in the freezer.

2. In a saucepan, combine milk, coconut milk, coconut, sugar and lime zest. Bring to a boil over medium heat, stirring constantly. Remove from heat and set aside for 30 minutes.

3. Strain mixture into chilled container. Place in freezer for 1 hour. Using a fork, scrape and stir cold mixture, breaking up the ice crystals. Return to freezer. Stir granita every half-hour for 3 hours, until texture resembles snow.

4. *Licorice Sauce:* In a saucepan, combine caramel sauce and cream. Cook over medium heat, stirring constantly, for 8 minutes. Remove from heat. Stir in jellybeans and aniseed. Set aside for 10 minutes.

5. Place a strainer over a bowl and strain sauce. Discard solids. Spoon about 2 tbsp (30 mL) into each jar and refrigerate for 30 minutes.

6. When you're ready to serve, spoon coconut granita into jars, dividing equally, and serve immediately.

Blue Lagoon Float

Sometimes the simplest recipes produce the most surprising effects. This is a recipe for people who love fun desserts and who want to surprise their guests.

Tips

Blue curaçao is an orange-flavored liqueur with added blue coloring. It can be replaced by Cointreau, Triple Sec, Grand Marnier or any other orange liqueur, including colorless curaçao. Blue curaçao has the advantage of being blue, which makes this dessert so unusual.

Vanilla syrup is widely available. Teisseire, Torani and Monin are common brands. Syrups are used to flavor water, cocktails, creams and coffee, among other things.

• Four 8-ounce (250 mL) tall jars

½ cup	blue curaçao liqueur (see Tips, left)	125 mL
4 tbsp	vanilla syrup (see Tips, left)	60 mL
4	scoops vanilla ice cream	4
2 cups	carbonated (soda) water	500 mL
4	maraschino cherries	4

1. Pour liqueur and vanilla syrup into jars, dividing equally. Mix with a long spoon. Add a scoop of vanilla ice cream to each jar.

2. In front of guests, fill each jar with ½ cup (125 mL) carbonated water, top with a cherry and enjoy.

Variation

For an after-dinner cocktail dessert, add a splash (1 oz/30 mL) of vodka to each jar.

Strawberry, Basil and Vodka Whiz

Remember your grandma's best strawberry jam? This is it — with, as a bonus, a splash of vodka and herbs to wake up your taste buds.

- Eight 8-ounce (250 mL) jars

3 cups	diced hulled strawberries (approx. 1 lb/500 g)	750 mL
1 cup	granulated sugar	250 mL
1½ cups	orange juice, divided	375 mL
2	packages (each 3 oz/85 g) strawberry-flavored gelatin powder	2
¼ cup	strawberry jam, strained	60 mL
12	basil leaves, chopped	12
20	large whole basil leaves	20
6	whole hulled strawberries	6
2 cups	vodka	500 mL

1. In a large bowl, combine diced strawberries, sugar and ½ cup (125 mL) orange juice. Cover and set aside.

2. In a saucepan, bring remaining orange juice to a boil. Remove from heat and stir in strawberry gelatin. Whisk in strawberry jam.

3. Drain diced strawberries, reserving juice. Transfer to a shallow pan and sprinkle with chopped basil. Pour gelatin mixture over strawberries and refrigerate for at least 6 hours or until set.

4. Place whole basil leaves in a pitcher or bottle. Add reserved strawberry juice, whole strawberries and vodka. Cover and refrigerate for at least 6 hours.

5. When you are ready to serve, cut jellied strawberries into small squares. Transfer to jars, dividing equally. Add flavored vodka, dividing equally, and serve.

Variation

A grind of fresh black pepper added to the vodka mixture adds a pleasant spicy touch to this dessert.

Fluffy Mimosa Extravaganza

The famous Grand Mimosa cocktail (orange juice, Grand Marnier and champagne) was allegedly invented in Paris at the Ritz, although the English lay claim to a version known as Buck's Fizz. This extravaganza transforms the legendary drink into a grand dessert. How chic!

Tips

To segment the oranges for this recipe, use a sharp knife to remove the peel and white pith from the fruit. Break into segments and, using a sharp knife, cut away and discard the white membrane, working over a bowl to capture all the juices. The resulting pure orange segments are often called suprêmes.

If you feel like splurging, use Champagne.

- Six 10-ounce (300 mL) tall or drinking jars
- Electric mixer

½ cup	softened cream cheese	125 mL
2 cups	confectioner's (icing) sugar	500 mL
1 cup	heavy or whipping (35%) cream	250 mL
3 tbsp	finely grated orange zest	45 mL
1 cup	freshly squeezed orange juice	250 mL
2 tbsp	sour cream	30 mL
2 tbsp	granulated sugar	30 mL
3	oranges, segmented (see Tips, left)	3
3 cups	sparkling white wine or ginger ale (see Tips, left)	750 mL
2 tsp	Grand Marnier or other orange-flavored liqueur	10 mL

1. In a bowl, using electric mixer at low speed, beat cream cheese. Add confectioner's sugar and cream and beat until very fluffy and thick, about 6 minutes. Fold in orange zest. Spoon into prepared jars, filling to halfway. Refrigerate for 30 minutes.

2. In another bowl, mix orange juice, sour cream and granulated sugar, stirring until sugar crystals have dissolved. Fold in orange segments. Add to jars, dividing equally. Add sparkling wine, dividing equally. Finish each jar with a drop of Grand Marnier. Serve immediately.

Library and Archives Canada Cataloguing in Publication

Jourdan, Andrea, 1956-
    150 best desserts in a jar / Andrea Jourdan.

Includes index.
ISBN 978-0-7788-0435-2

1. Desserts. 2. Cookbooks. I. Title. II. Title: One hundred fifty best desserts in a jar.

TX773.J675 2013   641.86   C2012-907530-2

Index

More Great Books
from Robert Rose

Bestsellers

- The Juicing Bible, Second Edition
  by Pat Crocker
- 175 Best Babycakes™ Cupcake Maker Recipes
  by Kathy Moore and Roxanne Wyss
- 175 Best Babycakes™ Cake Pop Maker Recipes
  by Kathy Moore and Roxanne Wyss
- Eat Raw, Eat Well
  by Douglas McNish
- Best of Bridge Slow Cooker Cookbook
  by Best of Bridge and Sally Vaughan-Johnston
- The Food Substitutions Bible, Second Edition
  by David Joachim
- Zwilling J.A. Henckels Complete Book of Knife Skills
  by Jeffrey Elliot and James P. DeWan

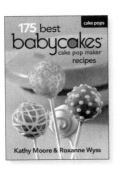

Appliance Bestsellers

- 225 Best Pressure Cooker Recipes
  by Cinda Chavich
- 200 Best Panini Recipes
  by Tiffany Collins
- 125 Best Indoor Grill Recipes
  by Ilana Simon
- The Convection Oven Bible
  by Linda Stephen
- The Fondue Bible
  by Ilana Simon

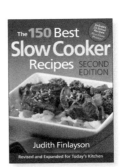

- 150 Best Indian, Thai, Vietnamese & More Slow Cooker Recipes
  by Sunil Vijayakar
- The 150 Best Slow Cooker Recipes, Second Edition
  by Judith Finlayson
- The Vegetarian Slow Cooker
  by Judith Finlayson
- 175 Essential Slow Cooker Classics
  by Judith Finlayson
- The Healthy Slow Cooker
  by Judith Finlayson
- Slow Cooker Winners
  by Donna-Marie Pye
- Canada's Slow Cooker Winners
  by Donna-Marie Pye
- 300 Best Rice Cooker Recipes
  by Katie Chin
- 650 Best Food Processor Recipes
  by George Geary and Judith Finlayson
- The Mixer Bible, Second Edition
  by Meredith Deeds and Carla Snyder
- 300 Best Bread Machine Recipes
  by Donna Washburn and Heather Butt
- 300 Best Canadian Bread Machine Recipes
  by Donna Washburn and Heather Butt

Baking Bestsellers

- 150 Best Cupcake Recipes
  by Julie Hasson
- Piece of Cake!
  by Camilla V. Saulsbury
- 400 Sensational Cookies
  by Linda J. Amendt
- Complete Cake Mix Magic
  by Jill Snider
- 150 Best Donut Recipes
  by George Geary
- 750 Best Muffin Recipes
  by Camilla V. Saulsbury
- 200 Fast & Easy Artisan Breads
  by Judith Fertig

Healthy Cooking Bestsellers

- Canada's Diabetes Meals for Good Health, Second Edition
  by Karen Graham
- Diabetes Meals for Good Health, Second Edition
  by Karen Graham
- 5 Easy Steps to Healthy Cooking
  by Camilla V. Saulsbury
- 350 Best Vegan Recipes
  by Deb Roussou
- The Vegan Cook's Bible
  by Pat Crocker
- The Gluten-Free Baking Book
  by Donna Washburn and Heather Butt
- Complete Gluten-Free Cookbook
  by Donna Washburn and Heather Butt

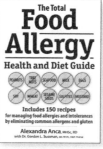
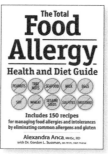

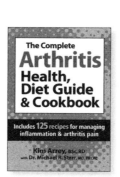

- 250 Gluten-Free Favorites
  by Donna Washburn and Heather Butt
- Complete Gluten-Free Diet & Nutrition Guide
  by Alexandra Anca and Theresa Santandrea-Cull
- The Complete Gluten-Free Whole Grains Cookbook
  by Judith Finlayson
- The Vegetarian Kitchen Table Cookbook
  by Igor Brotto and Olivier Guiriec

Health Bestsellers

- The Total Food Allergy Health and Diet Guide
  by Alexandra Anca with Dr. Gordon L. Sussman
- The Complete Arthritis Health, Diet Guide & Cookbook
  by Kim Arrey with Dr. Michael R. Starr
- The Essential Cancer Treatment Nutrition Guide & Cookbook
  by Jean LaMantia with Dr. Neil Berinstein
- The Complete Weight-Loss Surgery Guide & Diet Program
  by Sue Ekserci with Dr. Laz Klein
- The PCOS Health & Nutrition Guide
  by Dr. Jillian Stansbury with Dr. Sheila Mitchell

Also Available

Hardcover
ISBN 978-0-7788-0139-9
Softcover
ISBN 978-0-7788-0131-3

Hardcover
ISBN 978-0-7788-0140-5
Softcover
ISBN 978-0-7788-0137-5

For more great books, see previous pages

Visit us at www.robertrose.ca